MAKING YOUR OWN

CHEESE AND YOGURT

Making Your Own Cheese and Yogurt

BY MAX ALTH

FUNK & WAGNALLS
NEW YORK

Manufactured in the United States of America

ISBN 0-308-10081-6

2 3 4 5 6 7 8 9 10

Library of Congress Cataloging in Publication Data

Alth, Max
    Making your own cheese and yogurt.

    Bibliography: p.
    1. Cheese.   2. Yogurt.   I. Title.
SF271.A5 1973   637'.3   73-11111
ISBN 0-308-10081-6

Dedicated to
Char
Misch
Syme
Archie
and
Arabella

Contents

Foreword

Is it difficult to make cheese, yogurt, and kefir? Let me answer the question this way.

I made my first cheese quite by accident many years ago. We had just graduated from high school, two friends and myself. We took the forty-five hard-earned dollars the three of us had gathered over the winter, my father's old car and went off on a camping trip.

Enroute we stopped at a farm for several days, where we made a deal with the farmer. Early each morning he would leave two quarts of milk in a jar on a rock near a spring. Each evening we paid him twenty cents for the milk.

One morning we rose early to make a side trip up a little mountain. On our return that evening, we found that the waiting milk had solidified. Now, I had tasted soured milk before; we had it occasionally at home. But my companions never had and weren't about to. Except for what I could eat, the soured milk represented a dead loss. Our forty-five dollars had to see us up to the Adirondack Mountain State Park and back, a trip of about 700 miles. Twenty cents was a lot of money.

The solidified milk looked like cheese and it reminded me that cheese is made from milk, so I dumped the white goo into a clean dish towel and squeezed. The results had the consistency and appearance of cream cheese, but it didn't taste right. Nothing to lose now, I dumped salt in and mixed. That did it. It tasted fine.

We had the cheese for supper that evening and for the following morning's breakfast. We ate it with pumpernickel. My father was a baker. We brought along a seven-pound monster that lasted four weeks; good to the last, rock-hard crumb. To clue you on the date; retail, the loaf sold for 70 cents.

During the many years that have passed, my only contact with cheese has been gastronomical, I've eaten it.

So, to answer the questions, is it easy to make cheese, yogurt, and kefir at home? Yes. I'm not a dairy scientist; I'm not even a farmer. I'm a city fellow. If I can do it, so can you.

However, if you really, truly expect to read this book and run down to your cave and make your own Swiss, Roquefort, Stilton, Wensleydale, Camembert . . . . put this book right back on the shelf. You are not going to do it.

Don't feel bad. Lots of other people can't do it either and some of them are dairy scientists and some of them have tried very hard for many years.

You will, however, make excellent cheese that is as good as any you can buy and possibly better, because your cheese will be fresher and free from preservatives.

And I can assure you, even promise you, that your cheeses—at least at first—will be like no other cheeses in the world. You may want to make cheese like other cheeses, but don't be too disappointed if your Muenster comes out tasting a little like American and your American tastes a bit like Cheddar, or the other way round. And be prepared for cream cheese; you will make lots of cream cheese at first.

Cheesemaking is an art. Skill and control come with experience and an understanding of the principles involved. It is not too difficult. Sooner than you may believe possible at first, you will be packaging your own cheeses, proud to affix your label and give them away. Cheeses make lovely, inexpensive, and unusual gifts.

If you are like myself, the part you will enjoy most is the reaction you get when you persuade friends and guests to try your cheese for the first time. This is what almost always transpires.

At first they nibble cautiously, as if they feared poison. Then they actually taste a little. Then the dialogue;

"Made it yourself, eh? You didn't use a mix? Not bad, not bad at all."

At this point they notice and read my label, which usually surprises them further.

"You really did make this cheese yourself, didn't you?"

"Did your wife help?"

Although making cheese, yogurt, and kefir is not complicated, please do not jump to the recipes at the end of this book. You'll have no trouble making yogurt and kefir, which is a slightly alcoholic form of yogurt, but you may have difficulty making cheese.

Anyone can follow a cake recipe and come out with

something resembling a cake, but only an expert baker can look at a poor cake and state the cause of failure. The same is more or less true of cheesemaking. Read the entire book before you start and you will be on your way to becoming an expert. I want you to be expert and not disappointed, so please read it all first.

As for equipment, if you have a kitchen you probably have everything you need except a thermometer and an incubator (a warm box), which you can improvise cheaply enough. Some varieties of cheese can be made without an incubator.

You can make cheese in an hour or two, depending on the type. However, the process is spread over many hours and you will at first find it time-consuming. When you get the squeeze of it, you will be able to intersperse cheesemaking with your other pursuits. In a way, it resembles making some breads. You have to wait until the dough rises, but you need not watch the process. The actual work is negligible. Cleaning the pots is the hardest part. Waxing the finished, dry cheeses is the fun part.

A gallon of skim milk makes one to two pounds of fresh cheese. If you use milk powder to make the skim milk, total costs can be under fifty cents for the batch. Other cheeses are made from whole (regular) milk or a combination of whole and skim milk. A gallon of whole milk makes about three quarters pound of hard cheese.

In addition to milk you will need a starter, plus rennet and coloring for certain cheeses. These ingredients need not run more than a few pennies per pound of cheese. Thus, the cost of making cheese at home is pleasantly under the cost of purchasing it.

You will find this most satisfying if you have been

consuming the very expensive low-salt and low-fat diet cheeses. You can easily limit salt and fat content when making your own cheese. At the same time, you will eliminate all traces of adulterants and preservatives, which are unnecessary in homemade cheese and no need in store cheese, either.

Besides saving money and avoiding preservatives, you will have the satisfaction of accomplishment; the kind of pleasure one gets from building something with one's own hands or getting fruits and vegetables to grow. I imagine it is the same satisfaction one finds in cooking and baking. However, I think cheesemaking is even more interesting. You work with one of the simplest organisms known to man, the microbe. This single-celled living organism is so primitive it is classified as a plant and termed microflora. They are so small a trillion microbes can fit into a space about the size of a grain of corn. They are small and simple, but not entirely stupid. You have to keep your eye on them, which is part of the fun.

1

CHEESEMAKERS OF YORE
and nearby areas

If you believe the legend, cheese was discovered some six thousand years ago by a nameless Arab camel merchant. He was traveling with his herd, concubines, and servants from Ur to Eridu. One morning, among other tasks, he filled a leather bag made from the stomach of a sheep with milk. When the sun was gone at the end of the day, he settled his crew and prepared to enjoy a spot of milk, but in its place he found white lumps and a clear yellow liquid.

Ignorant of botulinus, the twenty-four-hour virus, and yellow fever and jungle rot, or perhaps simply indifferent, he ingested the curds and whey and was pleasantly surprised to find that the whey quenched his thirst and the curds, the white lumps, satisfied his hunger. Delighted, he ran off to share his discovery with his concubines.

Like most legends, there is a bit of truth in the story. An improperly or incompletely cured sheep's stomach contains a quantity of the enzyme rennet. (Actually, rennet is the lining of the stomach, and the enzyme is rennin. But since almost everyone calls the enzyme rennet, so shall we.) When rennet is combined with warm milk, the milk curdles and separates into curds and whey.

Actually, man became familiar with curds and whey as soon as he learned to draw milk from mammals and store it in pots. All milk contains bacteria, which cause it to ferment and then curdle when kept warm for a sufficient time—a day or so. Since animal husbandry began with the retreat of the last glaciers about eleven thousand years ago, we can place man's first encounter with curds and whey, a very simple form of cheese, at about this time.

The cheese fable contains another fallacy. Rennet does not make cheese; rennet curdles milk. The curd, or gelatinous white portion, that results is not cheese as we know it. Although it can be eaten as cheese, curd is not true cheese until it is cooked.

Cook milk curds and you have one of the "fresh" cheeses—cottage, Farmer, and the like. Add rennet to the milk before curdling and you can make hard cheeses such as Stilton, Cheddar, and so on.

Just who was first to cook curds remains unknown, but the first cheese may have been made by the people of Asia Minor during the fourth or fifth millennium B.C. The most likely area is Mesopotamia, where farming is believed to have begun. It was a land of wild wheat and barley, wild goats and sheep.

Mesopotamia is mentioned in the eleventh chapter of the Book of Genesis. "And it came to pass, as they journeyed from the east, that they found a plain in the land of Shinar and they dwelt there." The land of Shinar is the land of the people of Sumer, the Sumerians. This is where civilization is believed to have begun.

Sumerian clay tablets from about 4000 B.C. mention cheese. While the earliest tablets, written in pictograph, do not make such references, later tablets, written in cuneiform, do. A number of cylinder seals have been found engraved with pictures of a shepherd and his flock and rows of little circles indicating cheeses. In use the seal was rolled across a soft, smooth piece of clay; an ancient, little rotary press. Perhaps it was our equivalent of the rubber stamp and was a quick way of writing; send a dozen small cheeses by camel express.

As we wend our way forward in time, we encounter bits and pieces of information and artifacts relating to cheese. At the dairy of the palace at Mari, three hundred miles downriver from Ur, numerous cheese molds dating from the third millennium have been found.

Little pots for making cheese have been found in a Second Dynasty tomb at Saqqara, Egypt. These date from about 3000 B.C. Cheese is often mentioned in lists accompanying funerary offerings prepared during the time of the Old Kingdom, which existed in Egypt from 2800 to 2500 B.C.

Cheese is mentioned often in the Old Testament. Abraham was acquainted with butter, but modern translators replace the word butter with curds, believing this is what was intended.

In the First Book of Samuel, Jesse tells his son, David, "Carry these ten cheeses of kine unto the Captain in their thousands." Later, in Samuel, David is fed by Shobi, "And honey and butter and sheep and cheese of kine for David and the people that were with him to eat." David was carrying ten cheeses when he met with Goliath that fateful day.

Job, who turned a phrase as well as Shakespeare ever did, is credited with this line, and it still resounds, "Thou has poured me out as milk and curdled me as cheese."

It is believed that the art of making cheese was brought to Europe via Crete and the Greek islands by Near Eastern traders, possibly the Phoenicians who dwelt on the eastern shores of the Mediterranean Sea, not too far by land from Babylon. The Phoenicians were bold sailors, circumnavigating Africa in search of commerce. They established colonies on Cyprus, Rhodes, and other islands in the Aegean Sea.

The actual remains of what may well have been cheese dating from the Late Bronze Age have been found on the island of Therasia. And in Greece and Crete, fired-clay cheese strainers dating from the Neolithic and Early Bronze ages have been discovered. At the palace of Knossos on the island of Crete in the Mediterranean, south of the Aegean sea, tablets have been uncovered showing women grinding corn and men making cheese from the milk of either goats or sheep. The tablets were inscribed during the third millennium B.C.

Coming a bit closer to our age, we find the Greeks of the Classical Period were very fond of cheese and cheesecake. Their wedding cakes were usually cheesecakes, the best purportedly from a small shop on the island of Samos. On Delos, another island, coins were struck bearing the image of little cheeses on one side. And on the island of Argos, it was the custom for a bride to bring little roasted cheesecakes covered with honey as a special gift to friends of the groom.

Greek parents gave their children little cheeses much as we give our children candy when we forget the effect of sugar on young teeth.

A few ancient recipes for cheesecake remain. One was recorded by Athenaeus of Naucratis, a small city on the west bank of the Nile. He lived around 200 A.D., and is perhaps most famous for the fifteen books he wrote recording the conversations, food and table manners at a single banquet. Of the cheesecake he wrote, "Take some cheese and pound it. Put it into a brazen sieve and strain it, then add honey and flour, best made of spring wheat, mix it all into one mass and heat."

Another type of cheesecake, this one called *tuniai,* was deep-fried and then covered with honey while still hot.

Greek athletes trained for the original Olympics on a diet of cheese, and the Greek deity Aristaeus, son of Apollo, was famous for giving cheese as a gift. Even Zeus consumed cheese. His was a liquid sort called Opias. It was made of ripened milk curdled with the juice of figs, which makes for a bitter brew.

Homer, the bard of ancient times, sang of cheese. He sang of when Polyphemus returned, "He sat down and milked his ewes and goats all in due course, and then he curdled half the milk and set it aside in wicker baskets."

Draining cheese in a wicker basket appears to have been a common method in those days. The Greek word for baskets is *formos.* Latinized, it became *forma,* from whence derives the Italian word for cheese, *formaggio.* The early French called their cheese *formage* and later *fromage.* Our word for cheese derives from the Latin *caseus.*

In Roman times the most important city in Thessaly,

Hypata, was well known for its cheese and honey. So good was their product that it was distributed by traders.

Wherever the Roman soldier went, he brought cheese along as a staple of his diet. Light in weight, high in energy, it kept well in cool weather and could even withstand heat for short periods of time. And whereas dried and salted meat required preparation, cheese could be consumed directly as soon as the mold was removed.

The Chinese were also familiar with cheese, though its origin there is unknown to us. Marco Polo reports the use of a dehydrated form of cheese (or yogurt) as a common army food. Milk was heated to draw off the cream. The remaining skim milk was then thickened and dried to a paste by exposure to the sun. Soldiers were given rations of this "cheese," and each morning each man would place about one-half pound of the paste in a leather bottle and add water. When the bottle was shaken a thin porridge resulted. This was eaten as the main meal of the day.

Most of the cheeses we know today originated during the Middle Ages, principally in monasteries. Gorgonzola, Roquefort, Parmesan, Emmenthal (Swiss), and many others were first made a thousand years ago.

With the advent of the Renaissance, cheese fell into disfavor, and remained in low esteem for centuries. In Elizabethan times, physicians violently opposed the consumption of cheese. Shakespeare reflects this attitude in many of his plays. His characters refer to cheese with a degree of dislike.

In 1599, the Venetian senate passed a law making the sale or consumption of milk, butter, and cheese during a period of epidemic punishable by death.

Regardless of the real cause, more and more people

began laying the blame for their physical ills on cheese. Writings of the times reflect the general opinion.

In 1670, the English naturalist John Ray wrote, "Cheese is a peevish elf. It digests all things but itself." Another writer repeats a legend about a boy, born in a rocky cave near the peak of Derbyshire in England. As the tale runs the boy could digest pebbles. He ate the pits while others ate the fruit. However, he claimed, his stomach could not digest cheese.

To a large extent cheese was a mysterious substance. It was made of milk, which would sometimes ferment and curdle and sometimes not, or at least reluctantly.

Many people believed milk was soured by lightning and the evil eye. As lightning occurs most often on a hot summer evening and milk sours most quickly when it is warm, there is a connection.

The farmer and his milk maid, fooling around inside the barn, would see a flash—outside—and "zamee," the milk would be found sour in the morning. That milk would be sour later the following day, flash or no flash, appears to have been largely overlooked. The farmer's wife preferred a more direct explanation. She blamed it all on the milk maid and her evil eye. This is how the practice of calling other people witches began.

Humor aside, the medical history of man until recent decades is terrible to contemplate. Plagues swept up out of nowhere and destroyed thousands, and then disappeared as strangely and inexplicably. Man is a pragmatic creature; cheese made many individuals ill; so people stopped eating cheese.

The connection is quite valid. Cheese made from the milk of a diseased cow and *eaten fresh* will make the eater ill. Cheese made from milk taken from the same sick cow but permitted to age for more than two months will almost certainly (but not absolutely always) be wholesome. Cheese develops powerful antibiotic properties that kill most disease germs present, but the antibiotic, though always present in freshly soured milk, needs time to do its job.

There was no dramatic and sudden change in people's attitude towards cheese, but a very slow, gradual growth of renewed confidence. The difficult, laborious work that produced the change began when Anton Leeuwenhoek of Holland improved the microscope of his day and observed bacteria for the first time, probably in 1683. By 1857, scientists led by Louis Pasteur learned how bacteria caused milk to ferment. And in 1864, Pasteur went on to prove there was no such thing as spontaneous generation of life. In 1872 Robert Koch began his fight to convince the public that bacteria caused physical ills. The next year, Joseph Lister isolated the strain most frequently responsible for souring milk and named it *Bacterium lactis*. The lives saved by the work of these brilliant men and their associates cannot be counted. Meanwhile, as they used to say in stories over the radio, back at the ranch, people began buying and eating cheese in greater numbers. Pasteurization, the process that destroys bacteria without appreciably changing the flavor of milk, was introduced. The curve of worldwide cheese consumption took an upward turn.

Ever since Pasteur, Lister and Koch, cheese has found an increasing number of supporters. The per capita consumption in the United States and abroad continues to grow, especially in the past few years. Supermarkets now carry a greater variety of cheeses on their shelves than ever before. Specialty cheese shops are appearing everywhere, as are cheese clubs.

Each year we convert fifteen percent of all the milk produced in the nation into cheese—a staggering 2 billion pounds of it. Much is shipped abroad, since the United States is the largest cheese producer in the world. France is second, producing about half as much.

American cheeses, which include the Cheddars, are the most popular types in this country, followed by the cottage cheese types. In 1971, some 740 million pounds were consumed in the United States. Italian-type cheeses are also coming on fast in popularity. Our per capita consumption rate of all types of Italian cheese quadrupled over the period of the last twenty years. In 1971, each American ate 2.3 pounds of Italian-type cheese, much in the form of pizza, I would imagine.

Individually, the Swiss are world leaders in cheese eating, averaging 18 pounds per year. The Norwegians eat about 17 pounds per person per year, and the Swedes, Danes, Dutchmen and Dutch women, about 16 pounds. All these people as well as the Israelis regularly serve cheese with breakfast.

Among Americans, per capita cheese consumption increased from 4.5 pounds in 1929 to 8 pounds in 1956 and 11.5 in 1970. Some enthusiasts project a per capita cheese-eating figure of 20 pounds by 1980.

Along the way our taste in cheese changed. From about 1956 to 1962 we consumed increasing quantities of processed cheese. Although total cheese consumption has increased since 1962, the demand for processed cheese has remained at substantially the same level. It may be that we have grown flavor conscious, or it may be that we have become increasingly fearful of the preservatives usually found in processed cheese. Whatever the reason, our passion for natural cheese continues to grow. Incidentally, if you have been sedulously avoiding processed cheese because of the preservatives, I must warn you that some of the natural cheeses now contain preservatives. Read the labels.

In chapters following, details of cheese, yogurt and kefir, which is almost exactly the same as yogurt except for the small quantity of alcohol it contains, are discussed. In order that you may better appreciate the relationship between yogurt, cheese and cheesemaking a sort of "over-view" is herewith provided.

To make cheese, milk is coagulated. This may be accomplished by permitting the bacteria normally found in unpasteurized milk to multiply and produce acid which causes coagulation. When pasteurization has reduced the number of bacteria present, a selected strain of bacteria may be introduced into the milk to produce the acid needed for coagulation. And, the milk may be coagulated by adding a "coagulator" such as rennet, which is almost never used alone, but almost always with milk that has been "ripened" to some degree by bacteria.

When coagulated (or curdled, clabbered, clotted or soured—the terms are interchangeable), milk becomes a weak solid. Depending on a number of factors, there may or may not be a liquid present. It appears with time. When it does, the milk is said to have separated. The liquid is called whey; the solid portion is called curd.

When milk is coagulated by bacterial action alone (acid coagulation) it is sour and it is called yogurt or kefir, depending on the bacteria that did the job. The sour milk may be eaten as is or stored in the refrigerator and eaten later. Or, the whey may be poured off and the curd squeezed in a cloth. The resultant curd is sometimes called yogurt cheese and sometimes called cream cheese.

To make the familiar cheeses we are accustomed to eating, the coagulated milk is cooked to remove even more whey. Following, the curd may be squeezed, pressed, drained, salted, and eaten, or the compacted curd may be stored (aged) and consumed at a later date.

The soft, fresh cheeses are generally made by acid action alone. The hard cheeses are usually made with the aid of rennet. There are other methods, but the foregoing briefly describes the methods used for almost all cheeses. The resultant cheese is called natural. Some manufacturers add a preservative to extend the shelf life of their natural cheeses, and some add substances such as gum to their cheese to literally make them stand up better. For example, no-gum cream cheeses tend to flatten out when stacked in a showcase. Preservatives, gum or what have you added, these cheeses are still classified as natural.

Processed cheese is made by blending two or more cheeses. The end product is called processed, though it may not contain anything but the two cheeses. However, this writer knows of no processed cheese that does not contain preservatives and a host of other substances.

2

YOUTH BY THE GLASSFUL

In 1902, Elie Metchnikoff, a Russian-born biologist working in France, published a report entitled, *The Prolongation of Life.* Republished many times including an American version by G. Putnam's Sons, N.Y., 1908, his statements surprised and delighted the Western World. Man no longer needed to be satisfied with his traditional three score and ten years of life, but could now look happily forward with reasonable confidence to 150 years of active, healthy life. He had discovered the fountain of youth, and although it was running with soured milk, the results were the same: All who quaffed therefrom enjoyed improved health and long life.

Head of the Pasteur Institute in Paris, and because he won the Nobel Prize for Physiology and Medicine in 1908, his opinions at the time carried as much weight, if not more, than present-day statements by Linus Pauling, another Nobel Prize winner who strongly believes that massive doses of vitamin C provide an almost immediate, positive cure for the noxious, common cold.

Elie was convinced that most of us die prematurely and unnecessarily. In his search for the causes of early body failure, he visited many lands, particularly fascinated with materially poor regional and ethnic groups that reached old age despite little food, the paucity of medicine and severe discomforts.

He found the people in the general area surrounding the Mediterranean to be longer-lived than most, and amongst these people, the Bulgarians of that time, the poorest materially, of the lot, were by far most resistant to decay. He found 1,600 Bulgarians per million who were 100 years of age and older. In severe contrast, America, the land of milk, honey, money and supposed health, boasted no more than 11 (eleven—this is not a misprint) ancients per million on the average.

Instead of coming to the moral conclusion; riches breeds an early death, and poverty saves, he chose a more palatable answer: yogurt.

Mitchnikoff theorized that man suffers from auto-intoxication. Retained fecal matter and undigested food present in our intestines poisons our little bodies and an early death ensues. When beneficial bacteria displaces putrifactive bacteria, harmful, toxic bacterial by-products are not liberated in the intestines and not absorbed into the bloodstream. He was quite specific: Bulgarian health, abundant black hair and longevity was directly due to their consumption of yogurt. Said yogurt being milk filled with countless numbers of beneficial bacteria.

The People of the Mediterranean and especially the Bulgarians consumed tremendous quantities of yogurt. On an average, the Bulgars of Elie's day ingested nearly seven pounds daily. Seven pounds of yogurt works out to something like 12 standard 8-ounce glasses.

In support of his theory, Metchnikoff isolated the bacterium present in Bulgarian yogurt, proved that it was to be found in the intestinal tracts of their old people and that it did indeed supplant undesirable bacteria when eaten. He named the strain *Lactobacilli bulgaricus,* the organisms of long life.

Elie was so hep on his theory that he publicly proclaimed he would live another 100 years and began to devour large quanties of yogurt made with *Lactobacilli bulgaricus* every day.

The Bulgars who settled Bulgaria sometime in the 7th century after wandering across Asia were not the first to make yogurt a staple of their diet. Yogurt is an ancient food. It appeared unbidden and unassisted in warm climates and during the summer months in temperate zones as soon as man endeavored to store milk. All milk, as taken from the breast or udder of a mammal, contains bacteria that will convert it to yogurt, given warmth and time.

With experience man learned to encourage fermentation by adding a little yogurt to fresh milk or by storing fresh milk in containers, recently emptied but not washed, that had held fermented milk.

Yogurt is simply fermented milk. It antedates cheese by countless centuries. It was known as far north as the Scandinavian countries and as far east as China. The Mongol hordes that swept across Asia and most of Europe used to mix their yogurt with fresh blood taken a little at a time from the mares they either rode or led. They also smeared their faces with butter for protection against winter's blasts. They weren't neat, but then they did not have to be. They had just about everyone frightened nearly witless.

Metchnikoff was not the first to place his faith in yogurt's medicinal properties. Galen, the "wonder-working" Greek physician and writer, believed to have practiced medicine and penmanship from about A.D. 130 to 200, recommended yogurt to his over-indulgent patients. He told them yogurt was good for bilious and burning stomachs, that yogurt did not burn like milk taken directly from a cow.

There weren't many specifics to choose from in those golden times. Given a choice of frog-liver salad, ground unicorn horn or yogurt, his patients naturally opted for the solidified cow juice.

In India, yogurt, called *Dahi,* was considered food fit for the gods 2,500 and more years ago, even though other sour foods were believed to be dangerous and were forbidden.

In 679 A.D. a little printer in Damascus, which is not too far from the site of ancient Eridu, published what is believed to have been the first treatise espousing the value of yogurt. Entitled, "The Great Explanation of the Powers of the Elements and Medicine," it was a joint-authorship effort by some of the leading doctors of Greece, Persia, Syria, Arabia and India and a tech-writer brought in at great expense to edit the conflicting manuscripts. Arguments or not, the doctors took a definite stand, "Yogurt is good for strengthening the stomach and refreshing and regulating the intestinal tract."

King Francis I of France is reported to have paid a

fortune for a secret formula brought to him from Constantinople. When the secret of the formula was revealed, it was found to contain mostly yogurt. In France, yogurt is known as *lait de la vie eternelle.*

Yogurt was brought to America by immigrants from Eastern Europe and the Levant. Its first scientific mention was in a publication in 1875 by Dr. M.G. Dadirrian, who mentions studies on the effect of consuming yogurt, and encourages its introduction as a daily staple of the American diet.

Metchnikoff continued to eat yogurt and write books and papers for some 20 years, dying of old age in 1916 at 71, just 79 years short of his announced goal. This was a great disappointment to his supporters and even a greater disappointment to Elie. (Few of us scientists appreciate having our theories busted.)

Is there anything to the Metchnikoff theory that we die prematurely from auto-intoxication produced by putrifactive bacteria in our intestines? I'll give you the facts. Draw your own conclusions.

Yogurt, or fermented milk, is digested by the body in about one hour, whereas nonfermented milk, regular cow's milk, requires three hours of digestion by the average individual. Further, milk is not easily digested by all people. This may be a surprise to Americans who consume milk by the gallon.

Individuals who do not have a family heritage of adult milk consumption—and these individuals form the major portion of the population of the world—cannot properly digest milk after the age of four. And there are others whose families did consume milk for generations, but nonetheless cannot consume milk.

The cause of the difficulty is the shortage of lactase in

the susceptible individuals. Lactase is an enzyme that breaks down lactose (milk sugar). Because the bacteria responsible for converting milk to yogurt break down the lactose in milk, very little lactase is necessary to digest yogurt.

Milk is changed to yogurt, becomes sour and solidifies, as the direct result of activity by lactic bacteria. A glass of yogurt is in a very real sense a glass filled with countless desirable bacteria. We call lactic bacteria desirable and friendly because they destroy or inhibit almost all pathogenic (harmful to man) bacteria they encounter as well as some protozoa (microorganisms) that happen to be nearby.

When placed in yogurt, *S. typhi, S. paratyphi, S. paradysenteriae, Br. Arbortus, V. comma,* and *B. subtilis*—all pathogenic to varying degrees—are killed in an hour. In two hours, *S. pullorum, S. dysenteriae, P. vulgaris,* and *M. pyogenese* are killed; in four hours, *Br. alcaligenes* and *Ps. pyocyaneus*; in five hours, *E. coli* and *K. pneumoniae. S. lactis, C. diphtheriae, S. mitis, S. fecalis,* and *S. hemolyticus* live no more than twenty-four hours when immersed in yogurt. All are pathogenic.

Since cheese is made from milk soured to some degree, it also contains friendly bacteria and pathogenic varieties. To make certain none do survive, many states and a large number of foreign countries require that all cheese made from nonpasteurized milk be stored at least two months before being sold to the public. Such cheese is suitable for consumption even if the milk came from a diseased cow. Naturally, if the cheese is made from pasteurized milk, very few organisms are present and storage to insure against harmful bacteria is unnecessary.

Milk begins to display its antibiotic power as soon as

the lactic bacteria begin producing acid (that curdles the milk). A peak is reached about seven days after the onset of lactic acid formation, and in seven more days the antibiotic effect disappears. Nobody knows why, though the quantity of acid may continue to increase.

At its most effective moment, the antibiotic strength of yogurt is equal to approximately 0.06 penicillin units per cubic centimeter. In other words, an 8-ounce glass of yogurt is about equal to nine units of penicillin. This is true of all the many thousands of strains of lactic bacteria that can sour milk and the hundreds of strains that are presently used commercially and by home cheese- and yogurtmakers.

Metchnikoff's critics argued that Elie's favorite bacterium, *Lactobacillus bulgaricus,* could not be implanted, that it disappeared from the human colon as soon as said colon owner stopped ingesting *L. bulgaricus.* While this is true, no one has proven lactic bacteria must be implanted (take root–they are plants) to be effective. And other lactic bacteria, notably *L. acidophilus*, can be implanted. This strain of bacterium continues to flourish long after the individual stops eating yogurt made with the aid of *L. acidophilus.*

Although it is not essential to life that the human intestinal tract be inhabited by lactic acid-producing microflora (bacteria), the presence of this general class of bacteria has been proven important to health. Lactic flora produce an acid environment in which the bacteria of decay and other harmful microorganisms cannot flourish. (Remember, Metchnikoff postulated decay poisons the main cause of aging.)

It has been proven that the desirable intestinal bacterial

flora are particularly efficient producers of vitamins. They synthesize nine vitamins, including the B-complex vitamins and vitamin K, which is essential to normal blood coagulation.

In 1943, the American scientists Kajjar and Holt experimented with nine young men and proved that lactic bacteria did indeed synthesize vitamins, which were then absorbed by the human host. Antibiotic remedies taken by the volunteers destroyed the lactic bacteria, whereupon vitamin production stopped until the individual replaced the missing lactic bacteria by ingestion. Today, doctors often recommend yogurt to patients who have had to take massive doses of antibiotics.

A number of modern doctors, following in Galen's footsteps, recommend yogurt for a large variety of stomach-associated difficulties: hepatic diseases, nephritis, diarrhea, colitis, anemia, anorexia, eruction, distention of the stomach, flatulence. Others credit the use of yogurt with improved regulation of intestinal motility, suppression of pathogenic bacteria, improved digestion, improved hepatic function, and increased glycogen deposition in the liver.

Fermented milk is recommended as an aid to digestion on the basis of the change in milk proteins to albumoses and peptones, which are believed to stimulate hepatic and intestinal secretions. The lactic acid is viewed as a tonic to the nerves of the intestinal tract.

While various reports on the use of yogurt as an aid to health are in existence, they have not at this time been consolidated. No recognized agency has authenticated or rejected the use of yogurt. No one has made the exhaustive tests needed for a definitive answer acceptable to medical authorities. All we have now are a number of isolated reports by serious, dedicated medical practitioners and a large body of folklore.

People who eat yogurt regularly and enjoy it often recommend it for all gastro-intestinal disorders. Many of the companies manufacturing (growing) cultures for use in making yogurt often publish general recommendations along these lines. Some report yogurt relieves head colds. Others recommend warm yogurt in place of warm milk at bedtime. It is believed milk soothes the nerves of individuals shy on calcium and possibly other minerals; thus inducing relaxation and sleep. As yogurt is more readily digested, there is good sense to the suggestions. (Yogurt may be eaten warm.) Some advise yogurt as a cure for general lassitude and weakness, and still others report that daily consumption improves and regulates their bowel movements.

As can be imagined, Old Elie's death was a shock to everyone concerned, but all the disciples did not swear off the "white stuff." Isaac Carasso, a Spanish businessman, secured a quantity of *L. bulgaricus* and began producing yogurt on a commercial scale. He sold his product through pharmacies in Europe. With the advent of World War II, his son, Dannon, brought the culture to the United States and manufactured yogurt for consumption by Greeks, Turks, and Arabs in and around New York City. Later he dropped the longevity pitch and pushed flavor. If you are reading this book, you have probably heard of Dannon Yogurt.

At the same time, yogurt under the simpler name of sour milk has been made since 1910 by Yonah Schimmel on East Houston Street in Manhattan, and by others in New York and other cosmopolitan cities around the world.

Today, yogurt is available in many brands and varieties.

With the exception of types sold as sour milk or as pure and unflavored, all commercial yogurt contains additives. Whereas pure yogurt contains only milk—whole or skim—and bacteria, flavored yogurt contains a number of ingredients. Typically the contents label may read thusly: low-fat milk with 4 percent nonfat milk solids added, sugar, strawberries with potassium sorbate as a preservative, food starch—modified, milk protein, gelatin, artificial flavoring, artificial coloring, 1.6 percent butterfat.

Yogurt that has been pasteurized after manufacture and contains a preservative cannot contain many viable bacteria, since both pasteurization and preservatives destroy living organisms. Some always survive, but on the order of only 1 percent or so.

The therapeutic value of such commercial yogurt products must therefore be necessarily low. Further, since yogurt keeps well under ordinary refrigeration, the only reason for pasteurizing or adding preservatives is to prolong shelf life in the store. Because yogurt can be prepared from pasteurized milk, in which case there would be no pathogenic bacteria present when offered for sale, preservatives therefore have no reason other than extending shelf life.

Dieters often turn to yogurt in response to claims that particular brands have less than 1 percent butterfat. The statement, though true, is misleading. The butterfat content in flavored yogurts may be very low, but the presence of sugar and other high-calorie foods pushes the total calorie count up. For example, an 8-ounce glass of skim milk has about 75 calories; whole milk has about 150 calories. But some of the low-butterfat yogurts go as high as 268 calories per 8-ounce glass.

If you forget calories and count only carbohydrates you

will do much better, mentally at least. Plain, whole-milk yogurt has only 12 carbohydrate grams per 8-ounce glass. Skim-milk yogurt is higher because the butterfat, which is not a carbohydrate, is replaced by skim milk, which contains carbohydrates. Yogurt made of partially skimmed milk has 12.8 carbohydrate grams per 8-ounce glass, and yogurt made of skim milk alone about 13 or 14 grams. Commercial flavored yogurt measuring 268 calories per standard glass has 44.5 carbohydrate grams.

A table of calories and carbohydrate grams for yogurts and cheeses is to be found in the Appendix.

3

START WITH MILK

Cheese is made from milk, nothing else. Salt, color, spice, flavoring, pimento, lox—the list of substances found in cheese is very long—are all additives, nothing more. They modify the taste, vary the appearance or texture, but if the substance is not made from milk, it is not cheese.

Milk is an almost perfect food, very complex and very interesting. A quart of milk weighs a fraction more than 32 ounces. About 28 of these ounces are water. The balance of the quart, about four ounces, consists of proteins, minerals, lactose (milk sugar), milk fat, vitamins and trace elements. Together they are called the solids to distinguish them from the water. The solids alone, without the milk fat, are called solids-not-fat by dairymen, often abbreviated S.N.F. Milk fat is not called butterfat until it is changed into butter, though for all practical purposes, they are the same.

When milk coagulates, it is the casein that forms the curd. To a large degree the curdled casein may be likened to a sponge: When first formed it is very soft. With the passage of time the curd becomes firmer and all the liquid present in the milk is contained in the curd. There is no free whey. With the passage of more time, heat and applied pressure, the casein sponge shrinks and expels some, but never all of the whey. No cheese is perfectly dry.

Casein, the muscle-building protein, is a very strange substance. It is to be found nowhere in the world except in milk. It is not even present in the body of the animal, but appears only in the breast or udder of the mammal. In addition to casein's great value as a source of protein and calcium (casein is normally combined with calcium; it is called calcium caseinate), casein has many commercial applications. It forms a basis for glue, water-soluble paints, wallpaper and writing paper.

It is primarily casein, held in suspension much as fine clay is held in water, that gives milk and later cheese their white color.

All the elements present in milk remain in the milk when it coagulates. Nothing is lost by the act of coagulation. In fact, authorities believe that some of the vitamins are measurably increased when milk is coagulated by bacterial action.

As stated, there is a period of time in the life of curd when it encompasses all the milk present. With time, the application of heat or pressure, the curd shrinks. As it does, the curd loses water-soluble elements in the same general proportion that it loses whey. Nutrients bound by chemical or physical means to the curd remain with the curd and are found in the cheese. Elements dissolved in the whey remain with the curd in the same proportion that whey remains with the curd.

The rate and extent to which the curd shrinks depends on the nature of the milk (breed of cattle, time of year, feed), how the milk was coagulated (bacterial action, rennet), size of particles into which the curd was cut, cooking temperature and time length.

All curd shrinks when heated, rennet-formed curd most rapidly and to the greatest degree, acid curds (bacterial action) least rapidly and to a far lesser degree.

Rennet-coagulated cheeses such as Stilton and Cheddar retain from 50 to 60 percent of the milk's original calcium and about 50 percent of its phosphorus. The lactic-acid cheeses retain little more than 20 percent of the same two minerals.

Although the hard cheeses appear fairly dry, they, too, contain considerable quantities of whey, and with the whey, large portions of the many water-soluble vitamins found in fresh milk. Cheddar, for example, retains 26 percent of the riboflavin (sometimes called vitamin B_2 or vitamin G). Since fresh cheeses are washed in fresh water during the cooking process, they lose most of their whey and water-soluble vitamins. Cottage cheese, for example, retains little more than 2 percent of the riboflavin found in the original quantity of milk from which the cheese was made. Contrary to expectations, thiamine, another water-soluble vitamin (sometimes called B_1), remains in fairly equal percentages in both hard and soft cheeses. Both Cheddar and pot cheese, for example, contain about 15 percent of the original thiamine.

Since milk fat remains with the curd, we find a good percentage of the fat-soluble vitamins, A, D, and carotene (which is converted to vitamin A in our intestines) in the high-fat-content cheeses. Since fresh cheeses are most often made from low-fat-content milk (generally 1 percent milk fat), they are not good sources of these vitamins.

It might appear that with so much nutrient lost to the whey, advocates of cheese consumption are merely mouthing advertising implanted by television. This is not so. The value of cheese, however, lies in its concentration. To make 1 pound of hard cheese one starts with about 10 pounds of milk. (A gallon of milk weighs about 8.25 pounds.) Two ounces of American cheese, for example, began as two glasses of whole milk. Even if a percentage of the foodstuffs and vitamins is lost to the whey, few adults would drink the equivalent in milk of the cheese they eat (one 8-ounce glass of milk is equivalent to 1½ ounces of Cheddar cheese). And drinking milk or eating yogurt is the only practical, economic alternative to eating cheese.

We say, lost to the whey, but whey is not discarded. In commercial practice the whey is saved. Most of it is used for animal feed. Smaller quantities are used to make the "whey" cheeses, including Mysost, Ziger, and Ricotta. The balance of the whey is used as a food additive; you will even find it in some processed cheeses and cheese

Table 1. Typical Composition of Cow-milk Whey in Various Forms (in percentages)

Type of whey	Water	Protein	Content Milk fat	Content Lactose (sugar)	Content Lactic acid	Ash
Regular	93.0	0.9	0.2	4.8	0.6	0.5
Condensed	55.5	8.0	1.5	28.0	1.5	5.5
Dried	6.0	12.2	2.7	65.8	2.9	10.4

foods. Dried whey is added to human infant formulas, soups, candy, and cake.

At home the whey remaining from cheesemaking can be refrigerated and used for making a whey cheese.

Table 2. Percentage of Whey-curd Breakdown in Average Cheddar Cheese

Content	Whey	Curd
Water	94	6
Fat	6	94
Total solids	52	48
Casein	4	96
Soluble proteins	96	4
Lactose	94	6
Calcium	38	62
Vitamin A	6	94
Thiamine	85	15
Riboflavin	74	26
Vitamin C	94	6

Note: The whey is, of course, lost to the cheese. Each pair of numbers totals 100. The percentage of the original quantity remaining in the cheese is in the right-hand column, under curd.

So much for curds and whey. Let's get back to our original topic, milk.

Man has milked a great variety of mammals in his time, hungry men aren't fussy. The milk of the goat, sheep, cow, camel, yak, buffalo, llama, reindeer, ass, elk, mare, carabou, and moose have been consumed immediately as food and also converted to yogurt and cheese for considerable millennia.

Naturally the milk of the various mammals differs. The

Table 3. Approximate Composition of Popular Varieties of Cheese (in percentages)

Cheese	Moisture	Fat*	Protein	Content Ash	Salt	Calcium	Phosphorus
Brick	41	31	22	1.2	1.8	–	–
Brie	51	26	19	1.5	1.5	–	–
Camembert	50	26	19	1.2	2.5	0.7	0.5
Cheddar	37	32	24	1.9	1.5	0.9	0.6
Cottage							
Uncreamed	79	0.3	15	0.8	1.0	0.1	0.15
Creamed	79	4.3	13	0.8	1.0	0.1	0.15
Cream	54	35	7.6	0.5	1.0	0.3	0.2
Edam	39	23	30	2.3	2.8	0.8	0.6
Gorgonzola	35	32	26	2.6	2.4	–	–
Limburger	45	28	22	2.0	2.1	0.5	0.4
Neufchatel	55	25	16	1.3	1.0	–	–
Parmesan	31	27	37	3.0	1.8	1.2	1.0
Roquefort	39	33	22	2.3	4.2	0.6	0.4
Swiss	39	28	27	2.0	1.2	0.9	0.7

*Butterfat.

milk of the whale has a very high fat content. So far, whale's milk has not been made into cheese (you'd need one whale of a milk maid). The milk of the ass (donkey) has the lowest fat content. Although the milk of the camel is reputed to be most sweet, its lactose content is only 3.3 percent on an average. Human milk contains nearly 7 percent lactose, the highest of all milks. Bacteria feed on lactose, a disaccharide sugar, and convert it to lactic acid. They hardly nibble on anything else.

Table 4. Approximate Composition of Milk as Taken from Various Mammals*

	Content				
					Total
Mammal	Butterfat	Protein	Lactose	Minerals	Solids
			Percent		
Cow	4.0	3.5	4.9	0.7	13.0
Goat	4.1	3.7	4.2	0.8	12.7
Human	3.7	1.6	7.0	0.2	12.6
Mare	1.6	2.7	6.1	0.5	11.0
Ass	1.5	2.1	6.4	0.3	10.3
Sow	6.8	6.2	4.0	1.0	18.0
Ewe	6.2	5.1	4.2	0.9	16.4
Water buffalo	12.4	6.0	3.7	0.9	23.9
Camel	5.4	3.0	3.3	0.7	12.4
Reindeer	18.7	11.1	2.7	1.2	33.7
Whale	22.4	11.9	1.8	1.7	38.1

*Actual figures will vary with breed, time of year, animal's age, food, and general condition.

Mozzarella made from water buffalo milk is still available in most of Italy, though more and more Mozzarella today is made of cow's milk. When fresh there is little difference between cow and buffalo cheeses.

However, as the two age, the authentic *mozzarella de bufala* has the stronger, more distinctive flavor and aroma.

Roquefort cheese was probably well known before the First Century A.D., when it was praised by Pliny the Younger. It is made entirely from ewe's milk (lady sheep). Its characteristic bluish mold results when curd and moldy breadcrumbs are layered in the hoop and cured for about a month. Currently, better than 25 million pounds are annually produced in the caves of Roquefort, amidst the limestone waste lands of Causses in Aveyron, France.

A goodly, but lesser quantity of goat's milk cheese is also produced in France. In the main, French goat's milk cheese is devoured locally. Among the brands that reach our shores are Levrous, Valencay, Selles-sur-Cher and Crottin de Chavigol. Fresh cheese made of goat's milk has the consistency and approximate taste of ordinary cream cheese. But as it gets older, goat cheese develops a characteristic, hot-pepper-like sting, which, coupled with its ammonia-acid flavor, makes it readily distinguishable. It takes real courage to taste aged goat's cheese for the first time. Start out by tasting fresh cheese, and if you take enough time and work at it, you may get to like it. Many people do.

The milk of the goat is physically "softer" than cow's milk by 30 to 50 percent. This is one reason that goat's milk is recommended for invalids and infants. Like cow's milk, goat's milk can be purchased evaporated in cans.

Goat's milk is almost always white in color. It contains little carotene. This is a yellow pigment that is converted by the body into vitamin A. However, although there is little or no carotene in goat's milk, vitamin A is itself present in quantities proportional to that found in cow's milk. The cream in goat's milk is difficult to separate because the fat globules are too small. This is an easy way to distinguish between the two kinds of milk, assuming neither has been homogenized. Let them both stand. The butterfat will not rise to the top of goat's milk.

The characteristic strong odor and flavor of goat cheese and to a lesser extent, sheep cheese, is believed due to the presence of approximately twice as much capric, caprylic and caprioc acids in goat milk and somewhat less in sheep milk than in cow milk. The public has, however, erroneously attributed the pungent flavor and aroma to the smell of the he-goat in rutting season. Sheep are equally guilty by reason of association. There is no connection between the smell of he-goats and the milk produced by lady goats. The goat is a highly fastidious creature and very sensitive. When annoyed, she withholds her milk, thereby punishing the farmer who has angered her and pushing up the already high price of goat cheese. (Cows aren't as sensitive, but they too cannot be milked when excited or frightened.)

Smell is of course the major constituent of flavor, and one's nose is the most sensitive means of detecting and evaluating odor. It is calculated that we can smell an odoriferous substance diluted to one part in 23 billion. Our sense of smell is far more sensitive than our sense of taste and far more effective than the ability of any chemist to do the same with all his laboratory instruments.

Our taste perceptors are located mainly on the sides and base of our tongue and, in infants, on the soft palate and inner cheeks. Our olfactory area is chiefly in the uppermost region of the nasal cavity. The total sensitive "smelling" area is less than one square inch in size. We detect odors upon inhalation and most effectively when we do not breathe. Therefore, to really smell our best, we must sniff or whiff.

The flavor of a cheese, meaning its taste and odor, stems from the milk of the animal used as well as the method used in making the cheese. This is certainly obvious, but leaves us with the question of why cheese varieties, such as Swiss, for example, tastes different when produced in Switzerland and when produced in the United States and other countries. It certainly isn't for lack of trying. Swiss Swiss fetches a far higher price than Swiss made elsewhere.

In the case of Swiss cheese, a good part of the difference in flavor is traceable to the milk.

Milk as taken from the animal is called whole milk to distinguish it from milk with one or more constituents removed. When any quantity of the original milk fat is taken out, the balance of the milk is classified as skim milk. Store-bought skim milk usually has a fat content of 1 percent. Store-bought whole milk, called just milk, may

Table 5. Typical Composition of Genuine Buttermilk*

	Made From	
	Sweet Cream (percentages)	Sour Cream (percentages)
Water	90.8	91.3
Protein	3.4	3.4
Fat	0.5	0.6
Lactose	4.4	3.4
Ash	0.7	0.6
Lactic Acid	0.0	0.6

*Imitation buttermilk has a far greater lactic acid content, therefore it is sour.

Table 6. Average or Typical Composition of the Major Elements of Cow's Milk

Constituents	Percentage
Water	84.0
Milk fat	4.0
Casein	2.8
Albumin	0.5
Lactose	5.0
Minerals	0.7

Table 7. Average or Typical Composition of the Major Elements of Goat's Milk*

Constituents	Precentage
Water	87.4
Milk fat	4.0
Protein	3.0
Lactose	4.8
Ash	0.8

*There are more than 1 million goats in the United States. Some breeds produce little milk, but some, like the Swiss breeds of Saanen and Toggenburg, give 4 to 6 quarts of milk each day.

have a milk-fat content ranging from 3 to 4 percent. Some states have established minimum fat contents for whole milk ranging from 3 to 3.5 percent. Other states have not troubled to establish minimum requirements. For our purpose we assume a convenient 4 percent and let it go at that.

The milk fat content in cheese is just a little less than that in the milk from which the cheese was made. But don't figure that using 4-percent milk results in a cheese with a 4-percent milk-fat content. It doesn't work that way. Remember that very little milk fat runs off with the whey. Most of the fat stays with the curd. Start with 10 pounds of 4-percent milk and convert it to 1 pound of hard cheese, or soft cheese, and you end up with almost all the milk fat present in the milk. The 10 pounds of milk contained 0.4 pound of milk fat. A little was lost, so you have roughly 0.35 pound of milk fat in the cheese. Since the cheese weighs 1 pound, it is about 35 percent fat.

The fat content of milk is very important. The farmer gets paid for his milk on the basis of fat content. Milk fat (and lactose) is the measure of the number of calories present in milk, which in turn is a measure of the food energy present. Milk fat strongly affects the taste of milk. Richer milk, milk with more fat, tastes better to most people than milk that has been skimmed. And it is a mite easier to work with whole milk (4 percent milk fat) than skim milk (1 percent milk fat).

Milk fat (butter) is in itself very complex and fascinating. Although it is an oil, it doesn't run and spread like oil when heated. The reason milk fat, which when removed from milk becomes butter, doesn't behave like conventional oil is that it is composed of myriads of small globules, covered by very thin membranes. The membrane protects the globule from the action of various enzymes, including the one called lipase, which causes butter to go rancid. Just what the little sack is made of, nobody knows exactly. It is the sack that keeps butter fat from running like oil.

The size of the globule varies from mammal to mammal and from breed to breed, and from one animal to another of the same breed. Cow's milk, for example, contains as many as 100 million globules in a single drop. The size of each globule and how it combines with its neighbors to form clumps is important as this determines the viscosity of the cream—how easily it can be made into butter. Breeds of cattle that produce comparatively large quantities of milk have milk with large globules. When a cow needs to be freshened, the butterfat globules in its milk are very small.

Milk fat is composed of fatty acids and glycerol. Only some 12.5 percent of these will dissolve in water. Odors are absorbed by the water-soluble portion of the fat. The insoluble portion affects the hardness of the butter made from the milk fat.

My theory that the ready availability of cold storage favored and favors the consumption of butter in cold climate is somewhat supported by the people of Southern Europe today. These people eat comparatively little butter. In its place they consume less expensive, more easily stored, olive oil.

The Scandinavians are no longer international leaders in the consumption of butter. New Zealanders rank first. We are near the bottom of the list, but we eat more cheese than they do.

This might be a good place to say a few words on the subject of sweet cream. Sweet cream is the milk fat portion of milk. It is liquid when drawn from the cow and solidifies when its temperature drops below 92 degrees F. As fat is lighter than water, it rises to the top when milk is permitted to remain still. This is of little importance today when almost all milk is homogenized. This is a process that beats or mixes the cream so thoroughly with the rest of the milk that the cream never rises to the top again.

Sweet cream purchased in the shop is not all milk fat. Instead it is milk with a higher than usual percentage of milk fat. The name on the label indicates its fat content.

Light cream is at least 18 percent milk fat. In some
 states, fat content may run to 20 percent.
Table cream ranges from 20 to 25 percent fat.
Whipping cream runs from 34 to 40 percent milk fat.
Half-and-half is usually 10.5 percent milk fat but may
 reach 12 percent in some states.

But not too far back, when milkmen used a horse and
wagon to deliver milk in bottles before dawn, a housewife
could judge the cream content of the milk she purchased
just by looking at it. The cream would be on top, clearly
separated from the milk below.

Homogenized milk makes it a little more difficult to
make cheese. Curds formed from homogenized milk are
less firm than those made from non-homogenized milk.
You cannot de-homogenize milk. All you can do is try
different brands in hopes of finding one company that
homogenizes less vigorously than the others.

Do not confuse pasteurization with homogenization.
There is a spate of controversy over whether or not
pasteurization detracts from the flavor of cheese, with
many arguments on both sides. But when you use
pasteurized milk you need not worry over the possibility
of pathogenic (harmful) bacteria being present. If the milk
tastes fresh you can drink it and use it for cheesemaking
without fear, whether you are making fresh or aged cheese.
With non-pasteurized milk you are limited by health
considerations to aged cheeses. The effect of
pasteurization upon the firmness of the curd is minimal.
Non-pasteurized milk is not worth the trouble of searching
out, since you will probably have to procure it directly
from the farm.

We have given the average percentage of milk fat in
whole milk as 4 percent. This happens to be the average

milk fat content of cow's milk. The actual fat content varies widely from breed to breed and from cow to cow within that breed. Some breeds of cow deliver milk with no more than 1.6 percent fat on an average, while others produce milk as rich as 8.3 percent fat. Milk varies in color and fat content with the season. Summer milk has more color because the cows consume more fresh green food containing carotene, a yellow substance that appears in milk. Guernsey and Jersey cows have the yellowest milk of local breeds, while the Ayrshires and Holsteins have the whitest. The milk-fat content for all breeds is highest during the winter months when their milk is least yellow. So milk-fat content should not be judged by the color of the milk.

Milk flavor varies with the animal's diet. This is possibly the main reason why Swiss cheese cannot be duplicated elsewhere. In the winter, Swiss cows are fed on grasses dried in ricks placed in the sun. During the winter, American cows are fed grass stored in a silo, an almost completely airtight storage bin. In it the cornstalks, alfalfa, and other grasses (corn is a grass) undergo a chemical change not unlike that which takes place when milk sours. This makes the fodder more digestible but changes its flavor. Milk's flavor also changes when the cow eats wild onions, wild garlic, and noxious weeds.

The quantity of milk a modern, carefully bred cow produces is frightening. The amount is related to body weight and breed—the bigger the animal, the more she puts out. A Jersey produces about 12 times its body weight in milk or about 10,000 pounds annually. A Holstein produces about 15 times its body weight or some 18,000 pounds of milk annually. The goat produces about 18 times its body weight or about 1,800 pounds, and the sheep only three times its body weight or about 450 pounds of milk a year. This is probably the prime reason for the high cost of sheep cheese.

The milk of the various breeds of cow respond differently to the process of cheesemaking. Milk from the Guernsey and Jersey generally forms harder curds than does milk from Holsteins and Ayrshires. But there are usually several milk companies serving a given metropolitan area. Some may get their milk from different wholesalers, or from a different group of herds or a different homogenizing plant. Try the various brands. I have found the small-company brands best. The difference is worth looking for.

Buy the freshest possible milk. Check the spoilage date on the container. If you plan to use a bottle or carton for other purposes besides cheesemaking, don't open it until you are ready to make cheese. This will reduce the number of unwanted organisms slipping into your milk. Do not use milk that has been opened and stored a while in the refrigerator. The old farm cheesemaker's rule was, don't use milk that clabbers when you boil it. Such milk is very close to coagulation. I would not advise using any milk for cheesemaking that tastes even a bit off.

Converting milk that doesn't taste or smell "right" to yogurt, kefir, or cheese does not hide off-flavors. More than likely the end product will taste and smell worse after conversion than at the start.

On the other hand, if some of your sweet cream goes a bit sour, hold on to it. You can recover your investment and have a little fun by turning the cream into butter. You'll find directions in Chapter 8. The resulting butter will be the good, old-fashioned kind you can hardly get any more.

Before closing this chapter we need to discuss types of milk and cream you will be working with when making yogurt and cheese.

Besides fresh and powdered milk you will most likely be working with buttermilk. So let us first clear up a popular misconception about store-bought buttermilk.

When sweet cream is converted to butter it is churned—whipped or beaten. With time the globules of milk fat join one another and form ever larger golden clumps until there is a single bright-yellow mass—butter. The liquid remaining is slightly yellow and somewhat cloudy. This is true buttermilk and contains most of the water-soluble nutrients present in the milk and a small fraction of the butter-soluble elements. Buttermilk is comparatively high in phosphorus because churning separates the phospholipids from the fat globules.

True buttermilk can no longer be purchased at retail shops because it lacks uniformity in appearance, acidity, consistency, and flavor. The public doesn't care for a product that varies from week to week. True buttermilk is dried for use in pancake flour, animal feed, bakery goods, ice-cream mix, and other foods.

In its place the milk industry produces "cultured buttermilk," which is made by clabbering skimmed milk. That is to say, selected bacteria are introduced into the milk, which sours and curdles, forming yogurt. The yogurt is changed to a liquid by the simple expedient of stirring. In this form it is called cultured buttermilk. It is a good, wholesome and nutritious drink, but it is not buttermilk. It is shook up yogurt and has all the beneficial properties of yogurt.

To duplicate the appearance of true buttermilk some companies spray melted butter on the cold milk while agitating it. The butter has been prepared with more than the usual amount of coloring so that the specks of butter that form in the cultured buttermilk are highly visible. This type is called flake buttermilk. Sometimes rich cream is added to the buttermilk, after which the mixture is churned until butter globules form visible clusters. Sometimes the cream is churned until the globules begin to clump and then the cream is added to the cultured buttermilk.

Skim milk, which is milk with most of its milk fat removed, is used for making many varieties of cheese. Pot and cottage cheese are almost always made of skim milk. Farmer cheese may be made of either skim milk, whole milk, or some combination. Commercial cream cheese is made of whole milk to which some sweet cream is added. At home we can use milk with any milk-fat content desired, from skim milk through heavy sweet cream.

The hard cheeses we discuss, American, Muenster, and Cheddar, are usually made of whole milk, but can also be made from a mixture of whole and skim milk. To make this point clear: Mixing skim milk with whole milk or with sweet cream merely alters the percentage of fat present in the milk. Whole milk has about 4 percent fat; the skim milk we use has about 1 percent butterfat. Mix the two and you have milk with a fat content somewhere between the two figures given. The exact figure depends on the proportions used.

Assuming the whole milk you use has a milk-fat content of 4 percent and your skim has a fat content of 1 percent, mix in the proportions given below and you will have milk with fat contents as shown to the right.

Whole Milk (4%)		Skim Milk (1%)	1 gallon at
3 quarts	+	1 quart	3.25%
2 quarts	+	2 quarts	2.5 %
1 quart	+	3 quarts	1.75%

If your whole milk has a fat content of 3.25 percent (which is more likely) and your skim has a fat content of 1 percent, mix in the proportions given below and you will end up with milk having a fat content as shown.

Whole Milk (3.25%)		Skim Milk (1%)	1 gallon at
3 quarts	+	1 quart	2.7%
2 quarts	+	2 quarts	2.1%
1 quart	+	3 quarts	1.4%

Only the instant type of powdered milk is used. The noninstant kind sold to bakeries is not used. So far as brands of instant powdered milk are concerned, I have found very little difference beyond ease of mixing. The least expensive brand is a little more difficult to mix. The brands featuring the powder in neat quart packages are useful, but whether the higher price warrants the convenience is a personal decision. In some cases you will want to use a little more powder than that supplied in a premeasured packet. This of course nullifies the advantage of the measured package.

For our purposes permit me to state simply that the use of the phrase *powdered milk* means liquid milk made by adding one and a third cup of milk powder to sufficient water to make one quart. The statement, *Using a bit more*

41

powder, means adding milk powder to the standard formula to make the milk a bit thicker.

The milk powder we purchase at the supermarket contains enough fat to result in skim milk with a fat content of 1 percent. The powder is made by a process that effectively pasteurizes it, so you need not pasteurize powdered milk.

You may also work with sour cream, which can be used to make cream cheese. Sour cream is sweet cream that has been soured by the addition of selected bacteria; just the way yogurt is. Sour cream has an 18-percent milk-fat content.

Table 8. Approximate Composition of 1 Percent Liquid Skim Milk, Normal and Condensed

Ingredient	Standard skim milk (%)	Condensed skim milk (%)
Water	90.4	70.3
Protein	3.7	11.8
Fat	1.0	0.4
Lactose	4.5	15.1
Ash	0.4	2.4

Table 9. Approximate Composition of Supermarket Powdered Skim Milk

Ingredient	Percentage
Protein	35.51
Fat	1.02
Carbohydrates	52.0
Minerals	7.90
Moisture	3.51

Table 10. Vitamin Content of Supermarket Powdered Skim Milk

Vitamin	Percent daily adult requirement
1179 mg. calcium	157
934 mg. phosphorus	124
0.32 mg. thiamine	32
1.77 mg. riboflavin	147
1.05 mg. niacin	10
Vitamin A	50
Vitamin D	100

4

ADD CULTURE

Most of the cheeses we are accustomed to eating are made from "ripened" milk. Ripened milk is evening milk used in the morning.

"Allow four quarts of evening milk to ripen overnight in a cool place. Add four quarts of morning milk. This will make for a better tasting cheese than if you use all fresh milk. You may use either cow's or goat's milk: however, the milk must taste sweet. You cannot make good cheese from poor milk."

Should your antecedents fail to include a dairy farmer, the explanation is this: Cows are generally milked twice every 24 hours. Once in the evening and once in the morning. Evening milk is milk taken from the creatures at sundown.

How can you tell whether your carton of milk contains

evening or morning milk? You can't, but this doesn't matter. All milk sold today is effectively morning milk. It may have been drawn from the cow during the evening but it was kept cold so that it didn't "ripen." Powdered milk is also morning milk. Both must be ripened before they can make good cheese.

On the farm in the days before almost universal pasteurization, milk was ripened by simply letting it "set" a while, usually through the cool of an evening. Milk as drawn from a mammal contains a quantity of bacteria, which feed on the lactose and other nutrients in the milk. In return the bacteria produce lactic acid (sourness) and a number of organic compounds that contribute to the flavor of milk and cheese.

All milk, even when freshly drawn, contains some lactic acid, but the quantity is small, limited to 0.2 percent by federal law. We are accustomed to this small amount of acid and fresh, wholesome milk always tastes sweet to us.

Given time and a conducive temperature the bacteria feed and multiply, and the milk is said to ripen. Given sufficient time, the bacteria produce enough acid to coagulate the milk; in this semisolid state we call it yogurt.

Milk as drawn from a healthy animal contains bacteria that produce lactic acid and with it a flavor and taste we are accustomed to and like. When milk is pasteurized or dried, almost all the organisms present are destroyed. In the handling that follows pasteurization—measuring, bottling, etc.—other unwanted organisms slip in. The original, friendly, neighborhood bacterium, the lactic acid bacteria, are no longer present, or present in too few numbers to do much good. Milk is a vast ocean of food, ready to be gobbled up by whoever gets to it first and eats fastest. Usually it is a tie. Pasteurized milk that has been left too long in the refrigerator, or for a shorter period in a warm room, goes "bad" in popular terminology. The milk becomes filled with a mixture of "good" guys and "bad." The good guys produce the pleasant sourness we like in yogurt and cheese; the others produce gas, sweetness, bitterness, fruitlike flavors, a change of color or a spot of color, and sometimes cause the milk to overflow the container.

Should you incidentally ingest some "bad" milk, don't fret. The organisms you swallow are almost always non-pathogenic. In fact, in another medium, grape juice for example, the same organisms are more than welcome. The same yeast cells that produce gas and a sweetish flavor in milk turn grape juice into wine. Yeast converts a percentage of the sugar and other nutrients found in fruit juice into carbon dioxide and alcohol, which is of course the basis of wine.

The key to controlling bacterial content is culture. To control coagulation and produce the sour flavor in milk that we enjoy, we see to it that the particular bacteria we desire outnumber all other creatures in the milk. We do this by a process technically described as inoculating a sterile medium with a selected culture and incubating the same at an optimum temperature.

Actually, all we do is introduce the bacteria of our choice, called the culture, into the sterile medium, which in our case is pasteurized milk, and then incubate by holding the milk warm for a specific length of time. The process is called incubating because we are keeping the milk warm to encourage bacterial growth.

Basically, then, ripening results from adding some

To check your mother culture for coagulation and general condition, tilt the bottle gently. If it has coaged, you will see this. Coagulum in good condition separates easily and cleanly from the bottle sides. It does not stick. Its surface is shiny and bright. When acidophilus culture is used, the composition of the resultant mother culture may be lumpy and granular.

culture to pasteurized milk and then keeping the milk warm. Fortunately and unfortunately, it is not quite that simple. Unfortunately, because there are many little pitfalls and if you are going to be a successful little cheesemaker you need to know something of what goes on inside the milk. Fortunate, because the complexity of making cheese and controlling bacteria is what makes it all interesting. If cheesemaking was as simple as boiling water, there would be little of the satisfaction of accomplishment.

Bacteria are very small, very simple creatures, very active at their own temperature. Should you care to count you may find as many as 40 million to 100 billion microbes present in one gram of Cheddar cheese. (A gram is 1/453.6 of a pound.) Left to themselves, the organisms found in milk will double in number every hour and a half if the milk's temperature is approximately 80 degrees F. As the temperature drops they become less active: at 60 degrees F., they need four hours to double; at 50 degrees F., eight hours; at 40 degrees F., almost forty hours. That is why food doesn't spoil in the refrigerator. Cold does not kill many microorganisms. They continue to multiply, but slowly. Some strains can survive in liquid air, a temperature of approximately 310 below zero. They stay alive by shifting to their spore (seed) form.

Other types of bacteria can withstand above-pasteurization temperatures, which can reach 190 degrees F. None can withstand boiling.

Bacteria are classified and named according to their shape. The little fellas that are sort of rod shaped and rather long are called Bacilli. The round shaped organisms are called Coccus, which means seed or grain.

Bacteria multiply by dividing. That is the extent of their "fooling around." Tough, but that's it. Those that remain tied to one another after splitting are called streptococci. The round creatures that form clusters like grapes are named staphylocci.

Some arrange themselves into flat sheets. They are known to their associates as micrococci.

Bacteria are like people in that they have two names. Their first name is their genus or family name. Their second name denotes their personality or species. We work with bacteria belonging to the lactis family.

There are possibly thousands of different strains of lactic bacteria and probably hundreds that have been identified and are currently grown for use in making yogurt, cheese and kefir. How does one go about enlisting their aid?

Two ways. One can shop the local supermarket and purchase any milk product made with the aid of lactic bacteria. These include yogurt, cultured buttermilk and sour cream. Buttermilk is the most convenient of the three, but any of these products can furnish you with a complement of lactic bacteria. The trouble is that most of the lactic bacteria are defunct, having been destroyed by pasteurization and/or the addition of a preservative after manufacture.

Pasteurized products are usually clearly so identified on the carton. Preservatives may be so described or merely listed. There are many of them, with new ones added all the time. Some you may encounter include potassium sorbate, boric acid, sodium benzoate, sodium metaphosphate, and sodium citrate.

You can use buttermilk, yogurt or sour cream that has been pasteurized after fermentation or to which preservatives have been added as a culture, or starter as it is known. But, as most of the little creatures are in a sorry state, you have to use a lot more starter, and you still may fail, meaning time passes and nothing happens. Generally, if the milk does not coagulate satisfactorily after 24 hours and the medium (milk) has been kept at a suitable temperature, which can be anywhere from 70 to 118 degrees F.—depending on the bacterial strain, you are in trouble. The milk may eventually clabber, but you will have as many bad guys as good guys, which is another way of saying the final curd may be gassy, spongy, sweet, fruitlike, discolored, bitter, or a combination of all these undesired flavors and consistancies.

If you can locate nonpasteurized, nonpreserved cultured-milk products, you can use considerably less starter with far less chance of failure. So far I have been unable to locate such products, but they are worth searching for, if only to avoid the preservatives.

When a batch of milk goes bad, the best thing to do is throw it out right away and clean up afterward as thoroughly as you can. There is no known way of correcting or changing the flavor of unpalatable milk, since it is filled with all the organisms that turned it bad, so pour it right down the drain.

If you are going to use buttermilk or yogurt as a starter, and you might want to try them at first, try to find buttermilk that does not contain salt or rennet. It seems to work a bit better. Formulas provided in later chapters indicate the quantities to be used for making yogurt and cheese.

The use of store-bought buttermilk as a starter has one big advantage, as does store yogurt. It is handy to purchase and use. But there are disadvantages. As just stated, post-ferment, pasteurized and preserved products contain tired microbes, pooped from their hot bath, weak from withstanding their preserved environment. They will try their best, but one can't expect too much of them.

The major difficulty arises from the nature of pasteurization. It is not a "go, no-go" process.

Pasteurization destroys about 99 percent of the organisms. *About* is the key word. A slight change in the efficiency of pasteurization can affect a major change in bacterial count. Assume that pasteurization temperature is down slightly and instead of a 99 percent destroyed ratio, there is a 1 percent change. The ratio is instead, 98 percent. This would result in twice the number of viable bacteria in your starter. You would need just half as much starter but there is no practical way you could find this out.

Yet another disadvantage is that you must take the bacteria you get. I judge from the taste that the culture used for cultured buttermilk is a three-strain combination similar to that used for acidophilus yogurt: *L. bulgaricus, S. thermophilus,* and *L. acidophilus* in a ratio of 25, 25, and 50 percent respectively. This combination is not ordinarily used for cheesemaking. If the bulgaricus got out of hand, by reason of an overly-high temperature during incubation or an overextended period of storage, it could result in a very sour cheese.

The preferred alternative to using supermarket products is to purchase bacteria from a commercial dairy lab and make your own culture. The first batch you make this way is called the mother culture. The results, for a number of reasons, will be much better.

You start with happy, live creatures in specific numbers. The mother culture you make this way is a known quantity; there are no surprises and no disappointments. Commercial dairy labs offer a choice of bacterial strains, some suited to yogurt and kefir, some to the particular type of cheese you want to make. Cultured buttermilk can be used for cheese, but the results are not as good as with cultures literally bred for the job.

Although the initial cost is higher, the cost of starter made from lab-supplied bacteria in the long run is much cheaper per yogurt glass or per pound of cheese. It is also more fun.

You will find yogurt and kefir cultures for sale in health-food shops, a few drugstores, and a few farm-community grocers. I have not encountered any cheese cultures for sale in any of the foregoing, but then I do not live in a farm community. A cheese culture may be obtained by writing to the labs. You may secure the names of some local firms by writing to your state's agriculture department and asking for a list. Two that are interested in single-packet or single-vial orders are Rosell and Hansen's. You'll find their addresses and a few of their products listed in the Appendix.

All cultures sold in freeze-dried powder form are stored at low temperature; refrigerator or freezer as directed. When opened, the entire contents of the container must be used at one time and dumped into the milk. The milk is held at incubation temperature until the creatures have done their thing as indicated by the formation of curd. The milk is now filled with countless trillions of happy little fellas and is called the mother culture—from which all other succeeding cultures originate. The mother culture is stored in the refrigerator until needed.

Typically, Hansen's offers small quantities of many strains and combinations of strains of bacteria for making various types of yogurts and cheese. Hansen's calls its product DRI-VAC. A glass vial containing two grams of dried bacteria, a convenient quantity for home cheese- and yogurtmaking, sells for about three dollars, post paid for most strains. The vial may be stored for up to six months in the freezer or used anytime until then.

Recommended incubation temperatures vary from 70 to 118 degrees F., depending on strain or combination of strains. Cheese cultures are usually composed of several strains of bacteria. Generally, the cultures intended for making cheese are incubated at the low end of the scale, the yogurt cultures at the high end.

Hansen's recommends its cheese cultures be incubated at 70 to 72 degrees F. At this temperature incubation requires 16 to 20 hours. If you have lab-grade incubation equipment, fine. If not, I suggest you try for 75 degrees F. You will not lose as much in quality if your equipment drifts a bit than if you try for 70 degrees F. and drift lower. In the latter case, incubation time will be considerably extended, increasing the chance of encouraging other organisms in the milk.

By the same token, if you are using homemade equipment and the recommended temperature is 118 degrees F., try for 110 degrees F. This will greatly reduce the possibility of your equipment going over 118 degrees F. and the possibility of destroying some bacteria.

If no temperature is specified with the dry bacteria you purchase, use 85 degrees F. and you will not be far wrong. If no milk quantity is specified, use about a quart.

All bacterial strains slow their multiplication and digestive processes as temperature is reduced, but all strains do not slow down at an equal rate. For this reason, cultures stored in the refrigerator tend to change in composition with time.

Although the creatures slow down they do not stop. As they continue to multiply they continue to produce acid. With time the acid level increases. Some strains cannot tolerate acid levels higher than about 1.5 percent; they die off. Others, like *L. bulgaricus,* thrive in milks with acid levels up to 3 percent. This is why a composite culture including *L. bulgaricus* will grow increasingly sour with time. Eventually nothing but *L. bulgaricus* will be present. Fresh milk inoculated with this culture would be predominately *L. bulgaricus* when it coagulated.

To reduce change in the mother culture made from purchased bacteria, start with a relatively small quantity of milk—little more than will be used during the useful life of that culture—and keep transferring as it is used up.

If we so desired we could start a gallon of milk with our little vial or packet and with the gallon, start 100 gallons. Doing so would certainly return our $3.00 investment many times over, but where would we store 100 gallons of culture? If we could refrigerate it, most of it would have changed well before we used it up, if contamination did not end its useful life first.

I find a single-quart batch of mother culture about right for my needs. When something like two weeks have passed there is perhaps a cup full of culture remaining in my bottle. I use some of that to make a transfer and start another quart of culture going. If I have no immediate use for the old culture remaining, I eat it as yogurt.

In theory one can start with a single packet of dry bacteria and never purchase any more; just transfer from bottle to bottle endlessly. If you have an excellent lab, and not a dank little cave, and if you make a transfer with immaculate care every two days or less, you may be successful for a number of years. But at home, it will not work because of contamination.

When you first introduce the culture to the milk, when you remove culture for use, and when you make a transfer, the culture is open to the air. All sorts of undesirables sweep right in. And, of course, neither the bottle, the

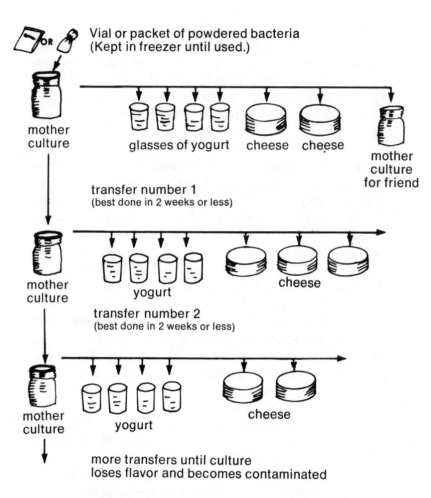

Vial or packet of powdered bacteria
(Kept in freezer until used.)

mother culture

glasses of yogurt   cheese   cheese

mother culture for friend

transfer number 1
(best done in 2 weeks or less)

mother culture

yogurt

cheese

transfer number 2
(best done in 2 weeks or less)

mother culture

yogurt

cheese

more transfers until culture
loses flavor and becomes contaminated

Let's propagate. How a vial or packet of powdered culture
is used to make initial mother culture, successive transfers,
and countless glasses of yogurt and buckets of cheese.

spoon, nor the milk is perfectly sterile. All harbor some microorganisms.

As contaminating microorganisms accumulate and as time passes, the bad guys become so numerous their handiwork becomes obvious. The culture doesn't work as fast as it did at first. Its taste and color are off. Tiny red spots will appear inside the bottle. When the culture reaches this stage it should be thrown out as quickly as possible. Clean up carefully afterward.

You can extend the useful life of your culture by limiting its growth during incubation. Remove the bottle and chill it as soon as a coagulum has formed. Don't let the creatures gorge themselves and run up the acid level right in the incubator. Should you let the culture remain too long at incubating temperature, the bacteria will run through almost their entire cycle, right then and there. The acid will quickly reach lethal bacterial levels and kill them. Store the culture at 40 degrees F., or as close as possible, but do not freeze. Culture cannot be frozen. By holding the temperature down, the period starting with coagulation and ending with high acid (and the beginning of the demise of the creatures) is extended. Remember that the onset of coagulation merely indicates an acid level. It is a convenient mark for people like us who do not actually take bacterial counts.

Keep your bottle of culture tightly closed. When you do have to open it, work fast and remove all the culture you may need at that time. Don't keep taking a spoonful at a time. And, finally, make sure that the spoon you use to remove culture has first been sterilized by boiling.

Commercial dairy plants have the same problem we have. They go to fantastic lengths to preclude unwanted organisms. Before they open a bottle of dry culture, they wash its top with a chlorine solution. They spray the walls of their work rooms with an antiseptic solution. The workmen wear special, clean clothes and boots. They wash their hands but do not scrub—I imagine the purpose is to prevent drops of water from flying about. The room is positively pressurized, which means there is a constant stream of sterilized air pumped into the room. When a door or window is opened, air flows out and not in.

Even so they run into contamination problems. To preclude a long shut down while the big vats are cleaned and new mother culture is grown, they store freeze-dried culture in sufficient quantities to inoculate 100 gallons of milk or more at one clip. This enables them to start up in 16 hours or less after they have had to shut down.

All this is to say, don't be surprised if you run into contamination difficulties and have to dump your efforts once in a while.

How much culture do you use to inoculate a given quantity of milk? Commercial cheesemakers use as little as 0.5 percent starter to inoculate a batch of milk. At this ratio half a gallon of starter would do for 100 gallons of milk. At home this would work out to about 1¼ tablespoons of starter to a gallon of milk. Thick starter is difficult to measure accurately, and at home, anything less than about 3 to 5 percent seems to get lost. You will therefore find my suggestions for starter quantities on the generous side.

With a pasteurized starter, such as cultured buttermilk, even more is needed. For best results it is advisable to use a minimum quantity of starter and hold the milk at incubating temperature a long time. This is not possible with cultured buttermilk starter, which is another reason it is not first choice for cheesemaking.

Another point to bear in mind is that coagulation by means of acid takes place when enough acid is present, regardless of how long it took. However, if too little starter was used, or if the starter was weak, which is effectively the same thing, the ratio between desirable and undesirable bacteria may be such that flavor is impaired.

It is necessary to mix the starter thoroughly into the milk. Bacteria aren't stupid, but they need help. They are microflora, members of the plant kingdom, but they have a kind of legs called flagellae. When they run out of food at one location they whip themselves about and move in the direction of lower acidity and higher nutrient levels. But how far can you travel when you are only 1/25,000 of an inch long?

The rate at which they split and multiply depends on the temperature of the milk. At 80 degrees F., almost all strains of bacteria double in number every hour and a half or so. One becomes two, two become four, and so on into the billions and trillions.

It would appear that the use of twice as much starter would cut the time to clabber in half. Starting with four microbes (four million would be a closer figure) instead of two, saves one multiplication step. While this is true, there are limitations. Time to clabber is reduced by increasing starter quantity and this is how commercial cheesemakers fix clabber time (so it is convenient to the night shift or something like that). They hold the temperature steady but vary starter quantity. However, you can't keep doubling the starter and cutting time to clabber indefinitely. Starter is already clabbered milk. It will not clabber a second time. It is not a glue that can be broken up into little pieces, dissolved in hot water and used again. Too much starter and there is no fresh milk left in the pot to clabber. Increasing starter quantity also increases lactic acid. This can throw your rennet calculations off.

For example, you may find that half a cup of commercial starter is just right for making American cheese to your taste. Switch to a cup of buttermilk starter and you may find the cheese a bit too sour, or that your rennet works too fast, meaning you have used too much for the percentage of acid in the milk. Yet commercial starter is more than twice as active as buttermilk starter.

The belabored point is, you cannot use any quantity of starter, you cannot use an unlimited quantity of starter to shorten time to clabber, and when you do change starter quantity appreciably you have to consider the effect of simultaneously increasing acid level.

Suggestions are made in Chapters 10 and 11 as to quantities of both commercial- and cultured-buttermilk starter to use for making yogurt and cheeses of various varieties.

So much for starter quantity. How about time? How long do you keep the milk at incubation temperature? While you wait for the little buggers to make acid?

We know bacteria double each hour and a half when kept at 80 degrees F. We also know that the greatest degree of change, that maximum bacterial growth, takes place somewhere near the end of incubation. The least change occurs during the first few hours.

So far we have limited our considerations to incubation at 80 degrees F. But we know that by changing incubation temperatures, we change the rate of bacterial growth. Bacteria multiply fastest when hot, slowest when cold.

The change in bacterial growth rate with temperature change is even more difficult to compute than the change in time to clabber with change in starter quantity. But we have a few fairly accurate bits of information and we can extrapolate the rest. (Guess is a better description.)

Roughly, very roughly, if you have a batch of milk and inoculate it with sufficient culture to bring it to coagulation in 23 hours when held at 70 degrees F., time to coagulation would be increased to 44 hours if incubation temperature was reduced to 60 degrees F., about 100 hours at a temperature of 50 degrees F., and more than 540 hours if the milk was held at 40 degrees F.

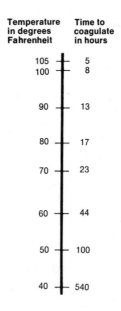

Temperature in degrees Fahrenheit	Time to coagulate in hours
105	5
100	8
90	13
80	17
70	23
60	44
50	100
40	540

An approximate guide for estimating the change in time required for incubation when the temperature is changed. For example, if the quantity of starter you used produced coagulation in 23 hours at 70 degrees F., the same mixture would coagulate in about 17 hours at 80 degrees.

Going the other way, the same starter and quantity of milk incubated at 80 degrees F. would coagulate in about 17 hours. Held at 90 degrees F., time to coagulation would be shortened to 13 hours, at 100 degrees F. coagulation would take place in 8 hours, and at an incubation temperature of 105 degrees F. only five hours would be necessary.

You needn't trouble to remember the numbers, all you need bear in mind are the following general rules:

Increasing starter quantity immediately adds more acid to the milk, shortens time to clabber, and may reduce the quantity of rennet needed.

Increasing temperature increases microbial activity, but not as much as decreasing temperature slows it down.

What is the immediate, practical value of the foregoing information?

Assume you have inoculated a batch of milk in the morning. You know from experience the milk will have coagulated and will be ready for cutting and cooking at seven that evening. However, when you uncover the pot, ready to cut and cook, you find no signs of coagulum. What went wrong?

If the temperature is down, you know what happened. If you know how far down the temperature is, you can look at the graph and estimate how far bacterial growth has progressed. If you set your warm box to 86 degrees F. and you find it at 60 degrees, you know that bacterial activity has barely begun. You can leave it at 60 degrees F. and figure that the entire time span necessary for coagulation will be approximately 44 hours. Or you can chill the milk to 50 degrees F. or less and start fresh the following morning, checking for signs of coagulation a couple of hours earlier.

On the other hand, if the temperature is merely down to 80 degrees F., you know a couple of hours more will suffice. You can, if you wish, raise the temperature to 100 degrees F. and possibly have time to complete your cheesemaking before retiring.

So far we have concerned ourselves mainly with the good guys, *Bacillus lactis.* Now a few, well chosen unkind words on the baddies. Remember, these fellows are not pathogenic. They are troublesome, not harmful.

The yeasts are probably the most ubiquitous. Like bacteria, they are single-celled organisms, either spherical or round in shape. Larger than bacteria, they are more readily observed under a microscope. They do not split, but give birth, usually, by a process of budding. Each cell becomes swollen and a lump forms on its surface. The lump grows in size until it is as large as its parent, whereupon it detaches itself. Sometimes the yeast cell develops three or four spores inside. These are known as ascospores. With continued growth the cell bursts and each spore goes on to become a yeast cell.

Yeast cells inhabit the very air we breathe. Wherever you find air, you find yeast cells. Yeast cells are to be found in milk, in comparatively large numbers in some types of Italian cheeses, and in old sweet cream, giving it a yeasty flavor. Some yeast strains form pink colonies on the surface of milk, cream, and moist cheeses. Other strains, called wild, can cause milk to have a bitter flavor. In sufficient numbers, wild yeast can do the same to butter, cream, and even cheese.

Molds are something else again. Unwanted mold can ruin a cheese by growing on its surface and inwards, causing spoilage. But some strains are desirable, and even necessary. Without the assistance of molds we would not have Roquefort, Gorgonzola, Stilton, and other mold-ripened cheeses.

In these cases, mold is injected into the body of the cheese by means of giant hypodermic needles. For cheeses such as Camembert and Brie, the mold is sprayed on the surface of the cheese.

Molds are much more complicated than the single-celled bacteria and yeasts. Mold usually begins life as a spore, which is somewhat like a seed. It sends out sprouts in the form of threadlike filaments known as *hypha,* taken by the way from the Greek word for web. Not content with a single hypha, the plant sends out a mess of hyphae, forming a tangled, fluffy mess called mycelium, taken from the Greek word for mushrooms. Molds and mushrooms belong to the same plant family, the fungi. Molds produce spores at the ends of their hyphae. These spores often give molds a distinctive color. Penicillin, an important antibiotic, is usually derived from penicillium mold, which often has a clear blue-green color. The same mold is used for ripening Roquefort, Brie, and other similar types of cheese.

Originally molds were grown with the aid of sour rye bread. Today molds are grown in dairy labs just like bacteria and can be purchased from the same sources.

Molds need moisture, air, and slightly acidic food, so cheese provides a perfect home. Since mold spores are spread by air currents, all cheese that is not to be mold-ripened must be protected from the air.

Molds on the surface of cheese grow inward by pushing their hyphae inside. The hyphae give rise to more spores and more hyphae. With time, mold can penetrate the largest cheese. As the mold digests the acid, conditions become unfavorable for the lactic bacteria and favorable for another type. When we select the mold and either spray it atop the cheese or inject the mold into the interior of the cheese, we call the new strain of bacteria's work delicious and lick our fingers; at least I do.

When the mold that settles on our cheese has not been selected, but came there by chance, the new strain of bacteria, encouraged by the absence of acid, is called putrefactive. The mold can be scraped off if it is confined to the surface, but if it has penetrated all the way through, the cheese is discarded. (Any portion of the cheese that is not discolored can be eaten.)

Sweet curd is another problem. It is caused by a strain of bacteria that produces an enzyme that coagulates milk with little or no acid present. In really bad cases, the milk will coagulate as with acid or rennet, but the milk will not be usable. It must be discarded. Farmers often refer to milk with a "touch" of sweet curd as milk with broken or bitty cream. It is often found in milk that has been held at 104 to 109 degrees F. for a length of time. Do not use such milk for yogurt or cheese.

There may be times when your culture does not develop the desired acidity or does not do so at the rate you believe normal. The inhibition may be due to traces of an antibiotic in the milk or a germicide such as a hypochlorite compound (chlorine) or a quaternary ammonium compound. But most likely it will be caused by the presence of phage—short for bacteriophage.

Bacteriophage is a virus that attacks bacteria. Seen with the aid of an electron microscope, they have a spherical head and a kind of a tail. Usually they confine their attacks to a specific strain or species of bacteria; at least one strain at a time. Thus, when a mixed culture is used, it is possible for one or more of the strains in the culture to escape destruction.

Phage is not a serious problem in the United States, where commercial cheese manufacturers use multiple-strain cultures and switch constantly from one strain to another in planned progression to keep the little phages off balance. Commercial culture producers supply their customers with rotational sequences of culture strains based on extensive laboratory testing.

When your culture works very slowly, when the creatures fail to produce their quota of lactic acid no matter how long you wait, there may be a chance you are in the midst of a phage attack. Don't panic. Don't run about your cheese cave, screaming the phage are coming, but do carefully check all your procedures.

. Have you kept accurate check of incubation time?
. Has the temperature remained where it should be?
. Is your culture too old?
. Did you add the quantity you thought you did?
. Did your milk get the "vibes"?

Perhaps we should explain the last suggestion first. If someone or something shook your incubated milk just before or just during the onset of coagulation, if the milk was vibrated, there will be no curd. Instead you will have cultured buttermilk. Check this out by tasting. If the milk tastes clean, sharp and sour, the bacteria are not at fault. Someone has been at your pots.

Assuming that so far as your records go none of the above has occurred, you still should run a test before deciding the problem is phage. A test is simple enough, but it has to be done with care or it's worthless. The test comprises no more than testing the activity of a measured quantity of the culture in question in a measured quantity of fresh milk—milk from a newly opened carton, or just made from powder, or repasteurized milk that has been in the refrigerator for a while. The test is conducted in a sterilized bottle that is sealed afterward and carefully held at temperature.

If the test milk takes a little longer to coagulate than usual, probably the culture is getting old. If the bacteria require one and a half times the usual number of hours or longer to do their job, it may or may not be phage, but I would dump the culture anyway. Any longer time probably indicates the presence of phage. The only certain test is when nothing at all happens; no acid growth, but it is best not to wait for that.

If the presence of phage is indicated, throw your culture down the drain. Wash all your equipment, sink, and tabletop with a solution made by mixing two tablespoons of household bleach (Clorox, for example) with a gallon of hot water. Let the spoons, cups, and pots remain in the solution for two minutes or more. Then rinse everything very, very thoroughly. Even a drop of chlorine solution will severely inhibit bacterial growth.

If you are throwing out culture merely because it is old and tired, you need not go through the chlorine drill. However, it is good practice to wash everything in the antiseptic solution once a month or so just to be sure.

Phage thrives in milk and milk products. This is why you should always clean your dishes, glasses, and hoops immediately after use. Handwash your cheesecloths in soap and water when you remove the cheese. Do not let them wait for your regular laundry.

Whether you dispose of culture because of fatigue or phage, follow it with a different culture. Doing so will reduce the possibility of phage ever putting your cheese factory out of commission. The Appendix suggests culture sequences. If you have been using one strain, as indicated by the manufacturer's number, follow that with another number.

5

COAGULATING

To make cheese we coagulate milk, cut and cook the resultant curd. Quite accurate, but about as useful as telling a person, you drive a car by pushing levers and turning the wheel.

Coagulation does not come up like thunder from Rangoon across the bay, but creeps up on milk much like old age sneaks into our lives. The curd is not cut so soon as it appears but some period of time after the onset of coagulation; preferably at a moment technically described as the isoelectric point. At this particular moment the curd is most firm, most responsive to the cooking process that follows.

Earlier and later the curd is less firm and less responsive. If cut too quickly or cut too late, more whey will appear in the pot. The curd will be more difficult to handle; more is lost while washing and draining. The texture of the final cheese is softer and there is less cheese. If cut much too late, there may be very little or no cheese at all.

Our goal therefore is not merely to coagulate milk, but to maintain control of inoculation and incubation to such a degree that we can accurately forecast the onset of curdling. Knowing when coagulation will start enables us to be on hand when the best moment to cut arrives.

When we don't know when the milk is going to begin to curdle, we have the choice of either hanging about and watching the pot or taking a chance we may uncover the pot too late. In a way it is like "making" a train. If you are off in your calculations and get to the station 10 minutes early, you can correct your error by waiting. If you arrive there 10 minutes late, no correction is possible. The degree of error was the same, but the results were entirely different.

Two methods are used to coagulate milk and form the curd necesssary to make cheese. One is called *acid coagulation,* the other is called *rennet coagulation.*

The first method involves inoculating milk with a selected strain of lactic bacteria and holding the milk at a temperature suited to bacterial growth until sufficient lactic acid has been produced to coagulate the milk. In this form, milk is known as yogurt.

The curd formed by acid alone is weak, delicate, and delicious. Acid coagulation may be used to make cream, pot, cottage, and Farmer cheese. The procedure is essentially simple. We wait until coagulation has begun. Then we conduct one or more tests, to be described, and when by these means we decide the curd is ready we attack it with our knife and cut it into small pieces.

The rennet method is more complex. Rennet is an enzyme, which is a substance that helps other organic substances to react. In a sense an enzyme is an organic "trigger." Rennet (actually rennin) is usually taken from the fourth stomach, or abomasum, of a calf.

Generally, commercially prepared rennet is a saline extract, which means it will be mixed with a little salt and may contain about 4 percent boric acid or sodium benzoate as a preservative. We purchase it in the form of hard, dry tablets.

Rennet is also available in paste form combined with lipase, another enzyme, which helps break down milk fat and is responsible for the special flavor of Italian cheeses.

Through the years effort has been expended to find a substitute for rennet, and although fig juice, pineapple juice and the extract of various plants such as Lady Bedstraw will cause milk to coagulate, little old cheesemakers still prefer the old stomach juice. Incidentally, fig juice makes for a bitter curd.

Rennet tablets can be purchased in many drug stores and some grocery shops. If asking for rennet confuses the help, ask for junket tablets. But don't accept a junket mix. It contains rennet, but a number of other ingredients, as well.

I use Salada and Hansen's Laboratory rennet tablets. And I suggest you start your cheesemaking using the same. Salada is a large, national company and I imagine you will have little difficulty in finding a local supplier. Hansen's is an old, international, dairy-biological supply house. It gives good mail service and you can purchase their products in local shops in some areas. The address of both companies are in the Appendix.

Undoubtedly, there are other equally reliable rennet sources. But the formulas given here are based on the rennet strengths found in these two brands. If you start with tablets of unknown strengths, you will have to experiment for a while to determine their strength. The rennet found in all tablets is the same for all practical purposes; the quantity differs.

Salada tablets sell for 48 cents a package of 12. Through the mail, Hansen's tablets go $3.05 for a tube of 25, postpaid. However, Hansen's tablets are 10 times stronger than the Salada tablets. You need to use 2½ Salada tablets in place of ¼ Hansen's tablet. Thus, the Hansen's tablets are considerably cheaper. However, while rennet tablets can be cut into quarters fairly accurately, it is difficult to cut them into eighths or smaller sections with any accuracy at all.

To measure off less than ¼ tablet, dissolve the ¼ tablet in a quantity of water and measure the water as desired. For example, to secure 1/16 of a tablet, dissolve ¼ tablet in exactly eight ounces of water (use a measuring cup). Two ounces of the liquid equals 1/16 tablet. While this method permits one to divide a tablet into as small a quantity as needed, it is wasteful since the dissolved tablet cannot be stored. It must be used or discarded.

It is important that the rennet be completely dissolved. To make certain, always use a clear glass and let the tablet sit long enough to soften up. They are quite hard. Always use cold water, and always use about ¼ glass of water when adding rennet to about 1 gallon of milk no matter how much or how little rennet you are using. If you have measured off 2 ounces of liquid rennet, add water. The quantity need not be exact, but it is important that sufficient water be used to permit thorough mixing and to avoid adding a concentrated stream of rennet to the milk. If you do, the rennet may possibly curdle the milk at one spot in the pot and leave the balance of the milk untouched. When adding liquid rennet, try to sprinkle it around.

There are several systems for adding rennet to milk in cheesemaking. For clarity, I have named them as follows:

. The *simultaneous method*—rennet is added when the culture is added.

. The *delayed method*—rennet is added sometime between inoculation and acid coagulation.

. The *short-stop method*—rennet is added one to three hours after inoculation.

The reasons for adding rennet when and in the quantities we do will be better understood after we discuss the nature of rennet and its response to temperature and acid. A better understanding of rennet will also enable us more accurately to predict the onset of coagulation (which saves on pot-watching time) and more accurately to pinpoint the moment of truth in curd cutting (which makes for more cheese).

When rennet is added to milk, coagulation occurs after a period of time. The speed and power with which rennet affects milk depends on the quantity of rennet added, the temperature of the milk, and the amount of acid (sourness) of the milk. Let's deal with temperature first. It's easy.

As the accompanying chart illustrates, rennet works most rapidly and effectively when the temperature of the milk is about 105 degrees F. When the milk is hotter or colder, the rennet slows down. For example, if you need one tablet when the milk is at 99 degrees F., you will need three tablets to do the same job with the temperature of the milk at 70 degrees F.

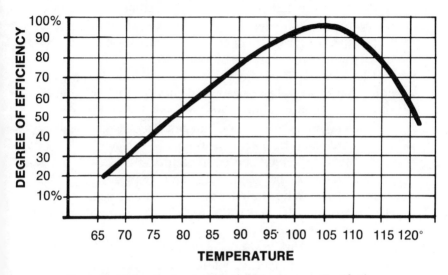

Rennet works best at about 104 degrees F. If the temperature is higher or lower, its efficiency or power falls off. If 1 tablet does the job at 99 degrees F., you would need about 3 tablets to do the same job with the milk at 70 degrees F.

The simplest way to get around the finicky nature of rennet sensitivity to temperature is to pick one incubation temperature and stick with it for all cheeses. Remember, the rennet is always added with the milk at its incubation temperature. Some pages back we mentioned that the curd is cooked after cutting. The process of cooking consists in raising the temperature of the curd. The increase may be as little as ten degrees or as much as fifty, no matter. Although there is a strong relationship between rennet quantity and cooking temperature, we always add the rennet with the milk at its inoculation temperature and we disregard cooking temperature, whatever it may be. Repeating, for ease in handling rennet, we stick to one incubation temperature for all our work.

I have chosen 86 degrees F. for all my work. It is a good compromise between speed and flavor. For maximum flavor use a lower temperature, but not below 70 degrees F. For maximum speed, you can go as high as 118 degrees F., depending on the bacterial strain.

So much for rennet and temperature.

The relation between acid and rennet cannot be dismissed as easily. Stated simply, the more acid present (the more sour the milk), the faster and more powerfully the rennet works.

At this juncture you may well ask, what is wrong with using too much rennet, or adding rennet when conditions in the milk—high acid level and more favorable temperature—are such as to speed its action and increase its power.

Lots. As stated previously, the curd is very soft at the start of coagulation. With the passage of time the curd becomes increasingly firm until it reaches a point when it is at its best. That moment passed, the quality of the curd, so far as cheesemaking is concerned, decreases rapidly. With time the curd becomes almost useless and sometimes completely useless for cheesemaking.

As the quantity of rennet added to milk is increased, the milk's reaction becomes faster and faster and the time span between the onset of coagulation and the correct moment to cut curd shorter and shorter. Given sufficient rennet, the milk will curdle right under the spoon. Even if it doesn't, too much rennet will result in a weak curd, far weaker than if too little rennet is added.

If conditions in the milk—high acid level and a more favorable temperature than anticipated—act to speed the rennet, the results will be the same. The curd will be very weak. In an extreme case the milk will look like cold water into which snow has fallen and frozen. The milk is coagulated but the rennet worked so powerfully and quickly that the casein was pulled right out of the milk. The curd tastes and smells fine, but the curd is in such tiny pieces that if you trouble to run it through a cloth, the little that remains will be a paste, edible but icky.

For convenience in discussion I have named curds of this type snow crystals and the area in which they are formed, snow country. Snow crystals are the result of over active rennet. They represent an extreme condition, easily avoided. But rennet action doesn't have to be this extreme to result in very weak curd and a serious loss of cheese.

If you look at the accompanying graph you will see that the area of increasing acidity is indicated by an arrow at the bottom. Curd hardness or firmness is indicated by an arrow pointing upward to the left of the graph. Time is indicated at the right. There are two lines in the graph itself. One indicates time to curdle. Note that it takes longest when the acid level to which the rennet is added is low. As the acid level increases, the same quantity of rennet curdles the milk with increasing rapidity. The second line indicates curd firmness. Notice that it rises and falls like a mountain's surface. The peak of this mountain is our goal. This is the point where the curd is most firm and most responsive to cooking. Technically, this is the isoelectric point.

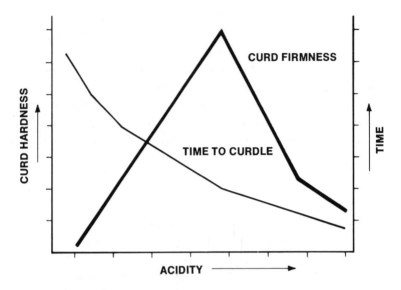

The line going downhill all the way indicates time—see left side of graph. As the milk becomes increasingly acid, as indicated at the bottom of the graph, the time needed for milk to coagulate with a fixed amount of rennet grows shorter and shorter.

The second line, which looks like a mountain, is related to curd firmness. The top of the mountain is where the curd is firmest. Notice that the peak is not where the milk is most acid, but where there is a moderate amount of acid, and where a moderate amount of time is needed for curdling.

The area to the left side of the mountain peak represents conditions that make for a weak but useful curd. The area to the right of the mountain peak also represents an area of weak curd, in this case curd that looks like snow that has fallen into water. Generally, such curd is useless for making cheese.

76

Note that the "mountain" peak is not at a point where there is the most acid and curdling takes the shortest time, but at a point roughly in the middle. Unfortunately, like most mountain peaks, while it offers the glory of success and a splendid view, it also offers one the opportunity to fall down.

If we were to make a series of tests we would find that as we either increased the quantity of rennet added or increased the acid present in the milk (the temperature remains constant) we would form curd more and more quickly and it would become more and more firm until we reached the peak. Once over the peak, any increase in rennet quantity or acid level would result in increasingly weaker curd and very quickly we would reach a snow country—the curd would be useless for cheesemaking. The left side of the peak is the safe area; the right side is the dangerous area—snow country.

All this sounds simple enough until you stop to consider that the acid level of inoculated milk in an incubator increases with time. Fresh milk, as regulated by federal laws, contains no more than 0.2 percent lactic acid. When the milk is inoculated and incubated, the acid level increases and the milk curdles when the acid level reaches about 1 percent. This is an approximate figure that varies with milks and temperature, but is sufficiently accurate for our discussion. In a large sense, one unit of rennet added to freshly inoculated milk, grows some five times in effective power by the time the milk coagulates some hours later. This is a tricky bit, especially as we have no means of measuring the acid level in our incubating milk.

We handle the changing acid level in two steps. First, we take great pains to keep inoculation and incubation under careful control. Second, we vary rennet quantity in accordance with our method of coagulation.

To review briefly, we use any of four methods to curdle milk. One is the acid-coagulation method; no rennet, the bugs are permitted to run their course. The second is called the simultaneous method; we add rennet at the same time we add starter.

The first method is used for high-acid, small-curd cheeses. The second method is used when we want to make the same kind of curd, but want it a bit firmer. In other words, both methods can be used for cream, pot, cottage and Farmer cheese.

In the simultaneous method, we start the same way; we add starter to the milk, and in addition, we add a very small quantity of rennet; typically, 1/16 Salada tablet, or less, to 1 gallon of milk at 86 degrees F.

In order to make high-acid, small-curd cheese, the bacteria must be allowed to run their course. This means that the action of the rennet must be such that it doesn't curdle the milk before the bacteria do. Since rennet curdles milk just as acid does, how can the little cheesemaker know his curd is truly sour? How does he know the curd is as sour as it would be if there were no rennet present? Or, who curdled my milk, acid or rennet?

Humor us, in the following imaginary cheesemaking procedure, by following directions and waiting for the explanation.

Measure out 1 gallon of milk (whole, skim, or a mixture). Place it in your cheesemaking pot. Add ½ cup commercial starter. Mix thoroughly. Remove ½ glassful of the mixture. Place the pot and glass side by side in your incubator; position them carefully in respect to the heat so that they both reach and remain at the incubation temperature which, let us say, is 86 degrees F. Now dissolve 1/16 Salada rennet tablet in water and add it to the pot of milk only. No rennet goes into the glass. Now we wait.

As we wait and watch, the bacteria in the test glass do their thing, as do the bacteria in the bucket. However, there is also rennet in the pot. Let us assume that the milk in the bucket coagulates first. How can we tell whether or not we have the desired acid level in the pot? Easy. We keep another eye on the milk in the glass. There is no rennet in the glass of milk. It will not coagulate until the acid level is correct.

The bacteria are active in both the pot and the glass. They will keep on working whether or not the milk coagulates—from acid or from rennet and acid. Thus, we can determine the acidity of the milk in the pot, despite the presence and action of the rennet, by watching the test sample for the onset of coagulation. Researchers at the University of Wisconsin's College of Agriculture, where the acid-coagulation (AC) test originated, suggest that coagulation be determined by running a knife through it. When a line can be seen, coagulation has begun.

In practice, we will vary the amount of rennet we add simultaneously with starter until the pot of milk reaches its optimum condition simultaneously with the onset of coagulation in the test sample. (This is why I call this the simultaneous method of making cheese, even though no one else does.)

Should you find that the pot coagulates well ahead of the sample, do not wait until the curd begins to separate from the walls of the pot, but cut and cook when ready. If you wait too long you will have a white lump floating about and very poor curd.

You will find that it will be difficult to judge rennet quantity accurately the first few times. If you add too little, you will have almost standard, small-curd, high-acid cheese. If you add too much rennet you will not be able to wait for the AC test to show a coagulum. The cheese that results will be large- or sweet-curd, a standard type of "fresh" cheese. The pieces are larger and not as sour as the high-acid type of cheese.

The third method of making cheese, the delayed-rennet method, can be used to make sweet-curd or large-curd cheeses and Farmer, Muenster, American, and Cheddar. A larger quantity of rennet is used and it is added to the inoculated milk hours after the start of incubation. Typically, ¼ Salada rennet tablet would be added to 1 gallon of milk approximately midway between inoculation and what would be the onset of coagulation, if no rennet were used. For clarification, assume that you use sufficient starter to bring a gallon of milk to acid coagulation in 10 hours at 86 degrees F. Rennet would be added to the milk about 5 hours after the start of incubation. The AC test would not be used. Instead the curd would be cut so soon as tests, which are to be discussed shortly, indicated it was ready. The delayed-rennet method makes for a firmer, less sour curd than the simultaneous or the acid-coagulation method.

The fourth, or short-stop, method uses even more rennet, as much as 10 times more. The rennet is added 1 to 3 hours after inoculation. This method is used for Muenster, American, and Cheddar cheese. It makes for the firmest curd and works so quickly that it is practical to omit the incubator and hold the milk at temperature atop a stove in a double boiler. However, as this method comes closest to the peak on the graph discussed earlier, it is also the one method most likely to lead you to snow country and failure.

By following directions carefully, the operation can be timed with sufficient accuracy to enable you to uncover your cheese pot some time safely before the optimum moment for cutting arrives with any and all of the four methods.

Swell. But how do we recognize the optimum moment to hack is upon us?

Over the thousands of years that cheese has been made, a goodly number of techniques for determining cutting time have been devised. The best requires that the curd be chemically tested. We don't have the equipment, so we can forget that. The next best is a timing system developed by the late Professor Kenneth M. Renner, head of the Department of Dairy Manufacturers, Texas Technological College. He suggested that when coagulating mainly by the addition of rennet (the third and fourth methods, the delayed and the short-stop methods) that the curd be cut 2½ times the number of minutes required for the onset of coagulation.

For example: Rennet is added at 10:00 A.M., first thickening appears at 10:20: 20 minutes were required for coagulation to start. Fine. Multiply 20 by 2½, which comes to 50 minutes. Thus, according to Professor Renner, the optimum time to cut this particular batch of milk would be 50 minutes after adding the rennet, or at 10:50. If the first signs of coagulation did not appear until 10:30, we would multiply 30 by 2½ to get 75 minutes. Added to 10:00, the time for cutting would be 11:15.

Another method for pinpointing hack time is called the Alth "Droopy Spoon" test, devised by yours truly. It goes this way. Some minutes before you believe coagulation to be due, the cover to the pot is removed and a clean teaspoon is used to remove a little milk from the edge of

81

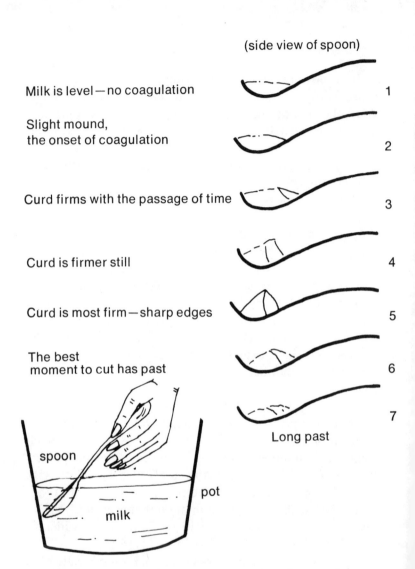

(side view of spoon)

Milk is level—no coagulation   1

Slight mound,
the onset of coagulation   2

Curd firms with the passage of time   3

Curd is firmer still   4

Curd is most firm—sharp edges   5

The best
moment to cut has past   6

   7

Long past

spoon

pot

milk

The Alth droopy-spoon test. Successive samples are taken from the milk at a point near the edge of the pot. The height of the milk sample and the sharpness of its edges indicate the condition of the curd. Sample sequence follows the number sequence shown above.

the pot. The milk so removed is discarded after inspection. Every few minutes following another sample of milk is removed, inspected and discarded.

Before coagulation, the milk in the spoon will lie flat. As coagulation begins, the milk will form a low mound. With increasing curd firmness, the height of the mound will grow and its edges will become more sharply defined. When the peak of perfection is reached, the mound of coagulated milk will be at its highest and the edges at their sharpest. As the optimum time is passed, successive samples will show lower and lower mounds of milk, less and less distinctly defined.

The advantage of the spoon test is that you can see coagulation coming up fairly clearly. The disadvantage lies in not realizing the optimum condition of the curd until the moment is past.

There is of course no reason why you cannot use both the Renner and the Alth tests together.

Still another, even more ancient technique is called the crooked finger or the clean-break test. One inserts one's washed pinkie into the curd and crooks it. If the curd is ready for cutting it will break "clean" across your finger. If you are finicky about using your finger, insert a table knife and lift its flat side up against the curd.

Trouble with the clean-break test is that some curds never become firm enough to break clean. All you get is a series of mush-ups.

Some dairymen lay the flat portion of a table knife on the curd and see how much of its weight the curd will sustain without giving way. Still others use a variation of the clean-break test, pressing down gently on the edge of the curd where it meets the pot. The curd is ready if it will

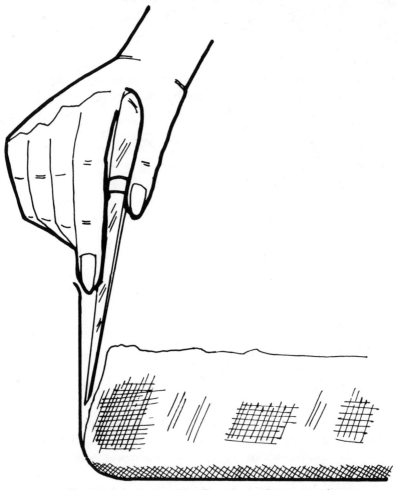

The breakaway test. The flat of a knife is inserted between the wall of the pot and the side of the curd. If it is ready for cutting it will be possible to pull the curd cleanly away from the pot.

break clean away from the side of the pot. Alternately, the flat of a knife may be inserted between curd and pot.

Yet another technique consists of observing surface whey. After coagulation has begun, drops of free whey appear on the surface of the curd. With time the drops form one very shallow continuous pool of liquid. The time just before the drops join is supposedly the best for cutting. I have never found this method accurate, but it is useful as a quick way of evaluating the curd.

With all these techniques it is always best to start cutting a little in advance of the optimum instant. If you are early, and with time you can tell by the feel of the knife and by whether or not the cut disappears so soon as the knife passes, you can always wait. If the milk is still in the warm box, little has been lost. With time the curd reaches its peak. If you have removed the milk from the incubator and placed it in the double boiler prior to, or even with the start of, cooking, still little will be lost if you cut early. The curd will simply come up to its prime a little faster because of the higher temperature.

To summarize, pay close attention to starter quantity, viability, and incubation temperature so that you always are ready with the knife well before cutting time. Be conservative with rennet quantity and time to keep on the safe side of the peak on the graph. Make your first cut a few minutes in advance of calculated optimum so that you can let the curd "ripen" up to you, rather than cutting late to find the moment has passed you by.

6

MEANWHILE, BACK IN THE CAVE

At 1:09 we take a sample of milk and make a bacterial count. If satisfactory, we hold the milk at 30 degrees C. until titratable acidity reaches 0.68 percent and the pH is 4.83. Rennet is added and when the isoelectric point of the casein is at pH 4.7, we cut the casein and commence cooking the curd.

If you really understand the foregoing, if you have a pH meter, microscope; if you know how to make a bacterial count and do the titration needed to measure percentage acid present in the milk you are a modern cheesemaking scientist and not welcome in my cave.

My cave is restricted to little old cheesemakers working with the same tools they had in the 1800's before the first cheese factory was opened in 1851 in this country.

It isn't actually a cave—wish that it were—but so far as

modern, scientific equipment is concerned, it might as well be. We have a thermometer, a clock and a fine, keenly trained little brain and precious little else other than pots and pans. That's about all they had in the good old days. Our only advantage, and it is a big edge, is that we know, more or less, what is going on and we are not troubled by witches. They are still trouble makers, but these days they do not spend their time hexing milk.

The big boys have the pH meters. In case you want to know, pH is the relation between hydronium ions, H_3O^+ and hydroxide ions, OH^-. pH can also be defined as equal to the negative exponent (base 10) of the hydronium ion concentration of a solution.

The isoelectric point of casein is the point at which the casein, locked into curd, has minimum hydration. At this time the curd will expel moisture most readily when heated. Since the expulsion of moisture and the firming of the curd is the purpose of cooking the curd, knowing the best moment to cut and cook is of course very important.

The big boys have autoclaves wherein equipment can actually be sterilized and not given a hot bath, which is sometimes just about the best we can do. Commercial cheese- and yogurtmakers have thermostatically controlled tanks that hold milk to half a degree of the desired temperature. Try that on your stove top.

But the "biggies" still goof. Until I started making my own I had been eating a particular brand of cottage cheese for years. The consistancy and taste of this cheese varied from week to week. Sometimes the curds would be large; sometimes small. The cheese in the one-pound containers differed in flavor and texture from the cheese in the two-pound containers.

This is the reason why the big cheesemakers push

processed cheese. They blend their way out of trouble. Too acid, too bland, too salty, no flavor; take a little of this and that, mix a dozen different cheeses together, and like the whisky bottler, you can end up with a standardized product.

I don't know the comparative costs between natural cheese and blended or processed cheese, but to make processed cheese natural cheese is shredded, tasted, blended, then heated and pressed into shape. That's a lot of handling after the cheese is normally ready for market.

Except for the presence of preservatives, there is nothing wrong with processed cheese as a nutritious food. The cheese foods are another matter. They aren't all cheese. You'll find anything and everything from dried whey to hominy grits mixed in. Read the label carefully sometime.

The general cheese-buying public is switching from processed cheese to natural cheese. After a decade-long boom, processed cheese sales have held steady. The percentage increase in cheese consumption in this country in the past few years has all been confined to natural cheeses.

Processed cheese has a lot going for it. The price is generally lower per pound. Processed cheeses are to be had neatly sliced and even packaged in individual slices, and the taste, if you like it, is so dependable.

The flavor and texture of natural cheeses vary considerably. Some gastronomes consider themselves fortunate if they encounter one excellent Brie or Camembert in half a dozen. These cheeses, high in butterfat content, are mold-ripened from the outside. They do not travel well and, like melons, must be eaten within a few days of their ripening. Other types of natural cheeses may exhibit less variation from cheese to cheese, but no two natural cheeses are ever exactly the same. The Swiss are possibly the most successful in maintaining a continuously high standard and similarity in their Swiss cheese. However, I have learned they also err. One reason for the close similarity of their cheeses, in addition to their tight control of manufacturing, is that they do not let the culls out of the country. They have men who spend their lives tapping cheese. The reverberations of the sound indicate the size and shape of the eyes (holes) in the cheese.

At home, variations in manufacture can be kept to a minimum by making the most of our simple equipment and by keeping in mind the actual nature of our work: We are bacterium farmers. Good yogurt-, kefir- and cheesemaking is to a great extent the art of bacterium control. Good control requires laboratory procedures that are neither complicated nor difficult. To a great extent we will follow in the steps of the great cheesemakers of yore. We will use similar equipment, but the important difference is that until the advent of Pasteur, Lister, Metchnikoff, and the rest, cheesemakers groped their way, literally in the dark. We have the benefits of modern science at our side.

The major reasons for the precautions and procedures observed in biological laboratories are the reduction of unwanted, intruding microorganisms and the maintenance of desired organisms in a healthy, happy condition.

Essentially it is a matter of cleanliness. This is not to imply your pots and pans are something less than perfectly clean. No doubt they are, but we need to be bacteriologically clean, and that is super clean or sterile.

We need to be most careful in the preparation, storage,

and handling of the mother culture because this is the starter from which all succeeding cultures are made. Thus, if we permit unwanted organisms to contaminate the initial culture, we will never be rid of them. Instead they will grow and multiply right along with our friends. With time the undesired microorganisms will grow to sufficient numbers to make their presence noticeable. When this happens we can no longer use the culture. We say it is contaminated and discard it.

There is little need to be as careful with inoculated milk when the resultant culture is to be consumed as yogurt or processed into cheese.

To postpone contamination (preventing it is impossible) we use sterilized containers and tools and reduce the culture's contact with air as much as possible.

A screw-top glass container is used for holding the milk that will be inoculated and incubated and stored afterward. Although the original "Mason" jar is now a collector's item and I believe the Ball company makes most of them now, the container we use is still called a Mason jar. Anything else that can be made airtight and immersed in boiling water can be used.

I find the quart size about right for my purpose, but as you can inoculate up to a gallon of milk with one packet or vial of dry culture, any size up to a gallon will do. Bear in mind that air enters every time you open the bottle of mother culture. If you plan on using no more than a few spoonfuls of starter each time, you may find that a gallon quantity is contaminated before you use it up. So judge your initial quantity of mother culture accordingly.

To sterilize the container and reduce the number of unwanted microorganisms, the following procedure is used.

The bottle, its cover, and its gasket are submerged in boiling water for a few minutes. If an air bubble appears within the bottle, roll the bottle over so that the hot water touches all parts of it. You will need a tool such as ice cube tongs for this procedure. Stand the tongs in the boiling water a few minutes so that the working ends are also sterilized. If you use a spoon, toss it into the water at this time.

After boiling, turn off the heat and let everything cool. Use the tongs to drain the bottle. Then set the bottle right side up on your worktable and place its cover right side down on top immediately afterward. Close loosely. Let your hands touch only the top, outside edge of the cover. When you are ready to pour the milk into the bottle, open, lift, and invert to drain. Until then, let it sit. Do the same with the spoon, if you have used one. Stand the tongs, open end down, upright in the pot filled with water that has been boiled. This will prevent the tongs' ends from becoming "soiled." You will need them again to retrieve the spoon.

Now to the milk, known in laboratories as the serum or the medium.

If you are working with acidophilus or acidophilus-yogurt culture, use skim milk only. Whole or skim milk may be used for any of the other cultures, including kefir.

If by some chance you are using nonpasteurized milk, it must be pasteurized. Doing so will destroy all the pathogenic organisms and the lactic organisms you may not want because they differ from those you plan to introduce. Pasteurization will encourage the growth of the culture you add. Since bacteria grow better in heat-treated milk. You may pasteurize milk by bringing it close to boiling temperature and holding it there for half a minute. The U.S. Public Health Service has established that pasteurized milk is milk held at 145 degrees F. for 30 minutes or 161 degrees F. for 15 seconds. The "flash" method is far more convenient for home use.

There is no harm in going over 161 degrees F., but if you allow the milk to boil it will rise up like an angry cloud and run over the pot unless you spoon like mad and cut the heat real fast. If you try to raise the milk's temperature too rapidly you run the chance of burning it, especially with whole milk. So heat very slowly and cautiously.

Far more than likely you will start with pasteurized milk. Should you pasteurize it a second time before using it as serum? I don't. I do not believe my equipment and technique permits me to do a better job than the local dairy. I believe I would not reduce the bacteria count in the milk by pasteurizing it a second time at home. Perhaps your equipment and skill is greater than mine. Even so, I do not believe the effort is worth the reduction that might result.

To keep my serum or medium as pure as possible I purchase as fresh a carton of milk as possible and I do not open the carton until I am ready to pour the milk into my sterilized Mason jar. I do not use milk from an opened container to make starter, although fresh milk from a previously opened container can be used without problem for making yogurt and cheese.

If you use skim milk for the mother culture serum, you have the choice of purchasing a carton of pasteurized skim milk or reconstituting your own from powder. I opt for the sealed carton of liquid skim milk. True, the process of preparing milk powder from liquid milk effectively pasteurizes the powder, but the water you add is not pasteurized and neither is the pot. In addition, air is bound to be in extensive contact with the milk, since mixing traps air. So, if you make your own skim milk for use as mother culture, you should pasteurize it. You need not do this when using powdered milk for yogurt-, kefir-, or cheesemaking.

Before we leave the business of home pasteurization, be advised that many of the yogurt culture packets advise boiling the milk prior to making yogurt and kefir. You will find that a 30-second boil, as suggested, will make for firmer curd. You will also be advised by some culture suppliers that a minimum of 3 level tablespoons of powdered skim milk be added to each quart of milk, whole or skimmed, when making yogurt and kefir. Both boiling and the addition of milk powder serve to make a firmer curd. Whether you prefer the slightly thicker curd to that obtained otherwise is a matter of personal preference. As I am guiding you through this cave, my opinion might just be desired on this subject: I don't think boiling the milk (whole or skim) is worth the trouble, but adding powder is easy enough. It does make for thicker yogurt.

Take note that although it is sometimes desirable to use more than the standard quantity of milk powder, when making cheese, the milk, whole or skimmed, is never pasteurized or boiled a second time. Heating the milk makes for firmer yogurt or kefir but weakens the curd for subsequent heating and converting to cheese.

With the pasteurization controversy settled, we carefully and slowly pour the milk into the bottle, leaving a couple of inches clear on top. If the milk is hot, we place the bottle, its cover fairly tight, in a pot of cold water. If the milk is cold, we use hot water.

While the temperature of the milk is being corrected, remove the freeze-dried culture from the freezer, which is the best place to store it, or the refrigerator, which is next best, and let it warm to room temperature.

For a quick check of the milk's temperature, hold the bottle in your hand. A few minutes' wait and a little gentle swirling brings the glass to milk temperature. If it is neither hot nor cold, it is close to body temperature, 98 degrees F. You can add the culture now or you can wait until the milk has reached the exact temperature you desire. To do this, add hot or cold water to the pot as necessary and measure the temperature of the water a couple of hours later. It takes about this long for the water in the pot and the milk in the bottle to reach thermal equilibrium. Measurements made sooner merely indicate the temperature of the water. The thermometer should not be inserted in the milk when the milk is to be used for mother culture.

If adding a packet of culture, the packet is shaken to make the creatures slide to the bottom, then snip the top of the packet with scissors and drop the contents gently into the milk. Screw the cover on tightly. If your culture is in a vial, rotate the vial lengthwise to loosen the buggers up a bit. Pry the tab up with a knife point and pull the cover apart without touching the open end of the vial with your fingers. When the cover is closed, the dry creatures, floating in a little mound of powder atop the milk, are mixed by swirling the milk around and around. Do not shake because that mixes air with the milk and we do not want air and its contingent of undesirables mixed into the serum.

Whether adding the contents of a glass vial or a packet, use the entire quantity at one time. Do not use half the dry culture and attempt to store the balance. It is unlikely that stored culture will be viable and contamination-free when you later try to use it.

The milk is incubated by holding the glass bottle in a bucket or pan of water, which is, in turn, placed in an incubator. The thermometer remains in the water.

Incubation temperature recommended by suppliers ranges from 70 degrees to 118 degrees F. The range from 70 degrees to 72 degrees F. produces the best balance between lactic acid-producing and citric acid-fermenting bacterial strains found in cultures blended for making many varieties of cheeses. The citric acid strains of bacteria, for example *Leuconostoc citrovorum,* produce diacetyle, carbon dioxide and volatile acids that help give cheese its flavor. Cheesemaking culture strains are best incubated at the comparatively low temperature of 70 degrees to 72 degrees F. On the other hand, the bacterial strains selected for making yogurt usually contain bacteria that are comparatively heat-resistant. These strains are incubated at higher temperatures because the culture companies believe the home-yogurtmaking public wants its yogurt in a hurry, because shorter incubation time reduces the possibility of contamination when little or no precautions are taken, and because the yogurt strains usually include some *L. bulgaricus* which thrives on high temperature and gives yogurt the characteristic sour flavor many people expect.

I suggest using 86 degrees F. to incubate all the strains you may use. My reasons are practical. Using home equipment, it is very difficult to hold a serum to 70 degrees to 72 degrees F. If your serum drifts higher, no problem, but if the temperature drops, incubation will be greatly extended and the chance of encouraging the growth of unwanted organisms and thus getting a short-lived mother culture is greatly increased. Short-lived because the bad guys are present in large number and will soon overrun the good guys.

Another reason for using 86 degrees F. with everything is that a simple warm box doesn't lend itself to easy temperature changes, so I have mine set for just one temperature and let it go at that. I do not incubate at 100 or higher because I have no need to reduce incubation time and I would seriously inhibit the citric acid-fermenting bacteria, the flavor bacteria as they are sometimes called. Eighty-six degrees is a good compromise. Perhaps incubation at a lower temperature would improve the flavor of my cheeses, I don't believe I could tell the difference.

In any event, the quantity of starter I use and temperature gives me a convenient schedule. Inoculate in the morning and cut and cook in the evening. A lower temperature would find me cooking and cutting in the early A.M.

If there are no instructions with the culture you purchase, incubate at 86 degrees F.and you will not be far off. Incidentally, if you incubate at a higher temperature and find the results too acid (too sour), incubate the following batch at a lower temperature. High temperature favors *L. bulgaricus,* which is very sour.

With mother culture we do not use the spoon or finger test to determine the onset of coagulation. The method used in their place consists of very gently tilting the bottle a fraction of a degree and observing the surface of the milk. If it doesn't flow, coagulation has begun. When this is barely but definitely discernible, the bottle of culture is removed from the incubator and stored in the refrigerator, preferably at 40 degrees F. or lower, but not below freezing. Chilling the serum at the onset of coagulation acts to extend the life of the mother culture.

Must any special precautions be taken when using mother culture?

Just a few. If you are going to remove culture with a spoon, sterilize the lower half of the spoon in boiling water. Do not put the spoon into the milk that is to be inoculated—in other words, if you remove a spoonful of culture from your bottle and add it to a glass of milk, do not mix the milk with that spoon and then remove more culture from your Mason jar.

If you plan to inoculate half a dozen glasses of milk, pour a quantity of culture into a clean cup, close the bottle of mother culture, and then use the culture in the cup to inoculate the glasses.

If you pour the culture out, take care not to let any drip backward on the neck of the bottle. If you do get culture on the bottle in a spot that will be covered by the cap, take a clean paper napkin and wipe the spot clean.

The first time you open your bottle of mother culture, remove more than you intend to use. It is important that you taste the freshly made culture. You may be surprised how much different "real culture," meaning pure yogurt, tastes as compared to the commercial product. You also need to know and remember the original culture flavor so that you can tell by tasting at a later date whether the culture should be used or discarded.

It also goes without saying that a spoon used for tasting should be discarded and replaced by a fresh spoon. Once a spoon has touched your lips it should be thoroughly washed, preferably in a dishwasher, before being used again. The dishwasher results in a more nearly sterile spoon because of the very hot water and the powerful detergents—too strong to be used with the hands.

This rule is always followed no matter the purpose of the milk. Makes no difference if the inoculated milk is to be consumed directly it coagulates, or is to be used to start more glasses of yogurt or kefir, or is to be made into cheese. In the latter case you may be mixing the curds and whey with your hands. No matter, the bacteria found in one's mouth are far more pernicious than those usually found on one's washed hands.

When you have almost used up the mother culture in your Mason jar you may be tempted merely to add milk. Do not do this. Most of the contamination present in the bottle will be found on its walls, which have greater surface exposure to the air than does the culture. That is why you will be able to inoculate a fresh batch of milk with culture taken from the bottom of the bottle, whereas milk added to the bottle will very often show early signs of contamination—gas, poor flavor, and so on.

So much for mother culture. What precautions are necessary with inoculated milk that is to be used as yogurt or processed into cheese?

If you are using the short high-temperature route and do not plan on using any of the yogurt to start more yogurt, ordinary care in keeping everything clean should suffice. If you are using 86 degrees F. or so, it is advisable to cover each glass or cup of milk with something or other. The small plastic bags are useful. Discard them afterward. If you plan to use some of the incubating milk to start more yogurt, cover the cups and glasses, no matter what temperature you may be using.

If you are making yogurt that is to be made into cheese, or merely ripening the milk, cover the milk container, preferably with a tight-fitting cover. As we have explained, the purpose of the cover is to reduce the incidence of intrusion by airborne microorganisms.

As you work you may spill a bit of milk now and again. It is essential that these spills be cleaned up immediately with soap and water. The creatures that give us the most trouble do so because they like milk as much as do the desirable bacteria. Each drop of milk unnoticed becomes the home of countless trouble-makers. A drop of milk inside the incubator provides a perfect home for such organisms. From here they can float up on a current of air and enter an uncovered glass or pot of milk.

Every now and again you will do well to clean your entire cave (working area) with a chlorine solution formulated from a couple of tablespoons of household bleach and a gallon of hot water. Wash everything, leaving the items washed in contact with the solution for at least a few minutes. (Do not get any on the walls and painted surfaces; they may become discolored.) Wash your milk bucket, pot, spoons, hoops (used for shaping cheese), followers, and weights (used for pressing). Then rinse everything thoroughly. Chlorine is very powerful. If a drop of the chlorine solution gets into the milk it will not coagulate. So keep rinsing and rinsing.

You may wonder why it is necessary to clean the hoops and followers with the chlorine solution. If you don't they will develop an odor that is transmitted to the cheese. Sometimes the hoop itself has no smell, but the surface of the cheese does. Laboratory cleanliness is a must in cheesemaking.

The thermometer should also be chlorine-treated from time to time. The thermometer enters all the solutions except the mother culture. Since it doesn't read above boiling, it cannot be sterilized by boiling, but it can be chlorine-solution treated. I rinse my glass rod thermometer after each use and dry it immediately with a clean paper towel, which I then discard.

Record keeping is almost as important as maintaining laboratory discipline. As we have been insisting on the simplicity of making yogurt, kefir and cheese, and as we have been feeding you the secrets in little, hopefully digestible, bits, the suggestion that record keeping is important may appear as another portion of the charade: The charade of calling my moth-eaten basement a cheese cave and referring to myself as a little old cheesemaker. I'm not old. Record keeping is not part of the fun, it is part of the work. As Little Egypt said to the gawkers at the Chicago World's Fair, "every little wriggle has a meaning all its own." Yogurt and cheesemaking is full of wriggles and each has a definite bearing on the outcome. For me, at least, there are just too many to commit to a weak memory. I note them down each time I inoculate a batch of milk.

For making mother culture, yogurt, or kefir, a record of the following data is suggested.

> Quantity of milk
> Type of milk—whole, skim, whole and skim, enriched (added cream)
> Milk treatment—pasteurized, boiled
> Milk additive—extra powder, coloring, flavoring, carrot juice, tomato juice, gelatin, fruit
> Starter—strain, manufacturer, quantity
> Setting temperature
> Incubation starting time
> Start of coagulation time
> Incubation to coagulation in hours

If you are making cheese, the following additional notes should be kept:

Rennet quantity
Time of rennet addition
Time to start of coagulation
Time curd is cut
Curd size (size of pieces into which curd is cut)
Curd quality
Start of cooking
Temperature rise (approximate number of degrees per minute)
Final temperature
Total cooking time
Curd quality
Curd washings—if done and number of times
Final curd quality after draining
Quantity of salt added
Size of hoop
Applied weight
Hours under pressure

The data will not help the cheese under hand but it will guide you in the making of succeeding cheeses. With experience, supported by your records, you will learn how each step in cheesemaking affects the final results. You will learn that you cannot guess when making cheese the way little old cake bakers appear to do.

Good bakers measure all the time. Watch old Granny. She takes a handful of flour and casually tosses it into the bowl—casually? Don't be fooled. Consciously or unconsciously, she is judging the mix; adding or subtracting to correct the condition of the batter. Unless you have a pH meter, unless you can measure the acidity in your milk, you have no way of knowing what is happening inside the bucket. All you can do is make corrections the next time around. You can do some juggling with the cooking, but you will be immeasurably aided in this if you have kept a record, especially until you get to know your way around.

In order that your notes have any value, all measurements must be carefully made. You may smile as you read this. "Careful measurements with a cup, a spoon and a four-dollar thermometer?" I'm not joking. I really do mean careful measurements. Our simple instruments are fine if used with care.

When you want 86 degrees F., make certain you reach that temperature. Don't settle for 84 degrees or 87 degrees F. The temperature will vary badly enough without your guessing at it. When you decide that four hours of incubation at 86 degrees F. is what you ought to try, take enough pains to make certain that is the time span and not the approximate time span. If you merely stab at the time, temperature, and quantity you are merely guessing. You may get good cheese if you are fortunate, then again, you may not.

7

ALEMBICS AND RETORTS

Most of my cheesemaking is accomplished with a mundane set of pots and other common kitchen tools. The two exceptions are the press and the incubator. Altogether you will need the following for making cheese:

Screw-top jars for incubating and storing culture
Nesting pots for a double boiler
Thermometer
Measuring cup
Colander for draining cheese
Draining cloths
Shaping hoops, followers, and weights
Incubator or some means of holding the milk at temperature
Press (mainly for making Cheddar)
Long knife
Long-handled spoon

As the screw-top jars and the reason for the tight-fitting covers have already been discussed, let's review the pot situation. Any pot excepting a galvanized pot or one of those nickel-plated pots sold in paint shops can be used. The paint pots are inexpensive and their shapes are convenient. But the nickel or tin coating wears off the second time they are cleaned and the milk develops rust stains. You will also find that pots made by bending the sides together have little cracks in which bits of cheese remain; they are devilishly difficult to make perfectly clean. Standard aluminum, stainless steel, and porcelain-coated iron pots are fine.

Pot size depends on the quantity of milk you wish to work with, and you may of course work with any quantity, but I find anything less than a gallon of milk an awful nuisance. Its temperature changes too rapidly. The larger the volume of liquid, the steadier the temperature holds; it rises and falls, but much more slowly. This means you can leave a large pot for a longer spell than you can leave a smaller pot. You need to "fool" with the heat less often. Bear in mind that temperature change in a gallon pot filled with milk is not half as fast as that of a half-gallon, but about one-fourth as fast.

Change in milk temperature in the absence of applied heat depends on room temperature. If you have heated the milk to 86 degrees F. and then shut off the heat, it will take hours for the milk to cool to, say, a room temperature of 80 degrees F. If the room is at 60 degrees F., the temperature of the milk will drop to 80 degrees F. in perhaps one-fourth the time.

Put into approximate numbers, if a gallon of milk at 86 degrees F. requires three hours to cool to 80 degrees F. in a room at 80 degrees F., the same amount of milk at the same temperature will cool to 86 degrees F. in an hour if the room is at 60 degrees F. If we start with a half-gallon of milk at 86 degrees F. in a room with a temperature of 80 degrees F., the smaller quantity of milk will cool to room temperature in probably less than an hour. In a room at 60 degrees F., the half-gallon of milk at 86 degrees F. will cool to 80 degrees F. in perhaps as little as 20 minutes.

When you purchase your pots, do not take the clerk seriously. Too many times the gallon pot he brings you will hold a gallon when it is filled to its brim. No good. You have to mix the curds and you need several inches of free board, space above the surface of the milk, if you are not going to splash milk or whey on your stove top.

If you plan to make no cheese but cream cheese, you can work with a pot of almost any size because cream cheese is usually not mixed after it is cut.

Since it is difficult, though not impossible, to control the temperature of a pot placed directly on the source of heat, be it gas, electric, or wood-burning stove, always use a double boiler.

Conventional double boilers are alright, but unless you get a very large set of pots, the top layer of milk in the inner pot may be well above the level of the water in the outer pot. As we work with moderately warm liquids, heat transport is almost entirely by conduction, in contrast to boiling water where the movement of the water transports heat. When curd forms, whatever liquid movement did exist is effectively blocked off. As a result, the milk and, later, the curd at the top of a conventional double boiler is always several degrees cooler than the milk and curd in the rest of the pot. You can feel this when you mix the curd by hand, and you can see the effect of the two layers of heat in the formation of curd. The effect can be most troublesome when the development of the visible curd is a half-hour or more behind the development of the invisible, warmer portion near the bottom. In other words, the isoelectric point of most of the curd has arrived and gone well before the visible curd appears to be ready for cutting.

Another objection to standard double boilers is the lack of access to the water in the outer vessel. The inner pot sits snugly in the outer. This is done to conserve heat and reduce moisture in the air. But this prevents us from measuring the water temperature in the outer vessel, and it is important we know the water temperature because it helps us judge the direction and to some degree the extent of temperature change in the milk.

For our purposes, we do best to select and combine individual pots. The inner pot should be large enough to hold the necessary quantity of milk we plan to work with and still have a couple of inches of space between the surface of the milk and the top of the pot. The inner pot should also have a tight-fitting cover. The outer pot should be at least an inch larger in diameter so that we can insert our thermometer in the water and so that the water volume is sufficient to hold the temperature steady. When the inner pot is filled with its quota of milk and positioned within the outer pot, the surface of the milk should be lower by an inch or more than the level of the water in the outer pot.

If you can find a floating milk thermometer, you have the best for the job. Failing that, a large, single glass rod photographic thermometer is fine. But it must be large and it must include a goodly length of scale from 70 degrees to 130 degrees F. You cannot use a candy thermometer because it will hardly move over the range mentioned; you cannot use a wall thermometer because the markings are

Hold that temperature. You need a fair quality thermometer with a run of marks between, say, 75 degrees and 130 degrees F. If you can't read the scale clearly to two degrees and have enough space between markers to estimate to one degree, you will find yourself way off without knowing it.

The temperature of the milk that has been inoculated for the purpose of making mother culture is never measured directly. Instead, the Mason jar is placed in a pot of water and the temperature of the water is measured. For accurate measurement, several hours must be permitted to pass so that the water and milk are stabilized at the same temperature. For convenience in temperature measurement, the Mason jar is held in the water during incubation.

too close. There should be no more than two degrees to each mark, and enough space between them so that you can estimate to at least one degree.

Why so accurate? Well, if you can actually read to one degree and the thermometer is off by plus or minus one degree, you can't be in very bad shape. If the closest you can read is to within five degrees, you could be off just one mark on the scale and be better than five degrees away, which is considerable for this kind of work.

Any kind of colander will do, even the plastic types. You may use cheesecloth if you wish, but I find it is not strong enough. I prefer well-washed muslin, which is stronger. Well-washed in this case means muslin that has been washed so many times that all the starch and filler are out and the cloth is soft.

Hoops, followers, weights, presses, and levers are discussed in Chapter 12, so there is no need to cover these pieces of equipment here.

And thus we come to incubation, the problem of holding inoculated milk at a desired temperature for a definite length of time.

The stability of the incubator or incubation system necessary depends on what will be done with the inoculated milk when the incubation period is complete. If you are making yogurt from a cultured starter (store yogurt or the like), and if you plan to consume it as yogurt, there is little need for thermal stability. A swing of ten degrees and even more is of little importance. The resulting yogurt may be a little soft or overly sour, but it is still yogurt.

People who just want yogurt and don't mind a little variation in taste and texture have evolved any number of incubation systems using nothing more than what they presently have at home.

Some of the simple methods include:

Placing the glasses of milk, covered with a paper napkin or the like, at the top rear of their refrigerator.

Placing the glasses of milk in a pan of warm water and covering the pan and glasses with several towels.

Placing the glasses of milk in a pan of warm water above the pilot light on a gas stove (you can feel the warm spot with your hand). Use an inverted pan to cover the glasses. Do not use towels atop the stove.

Placing the milk inside a gas or electric stove with the front door opened, control set to warm.

Top of the stove for you. This will work only on a gas stove that has a pilot light on top. Fill a baking pan with hot water. Set the glasses of serum in the water and then another pan on top. After incubation be certain to wash the pans very carefully since any spilled milk will attract bacteria.

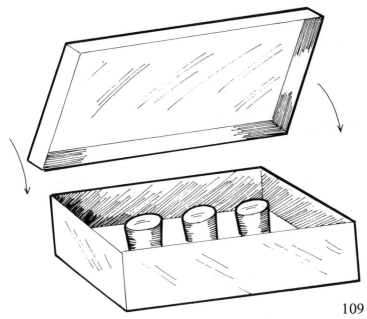

Placing the milk inside an electric stove along with a large bucket of hot water. Cover the milk and keep the stove door closed. As the stove is insulated, the milk will remain warm for a long time. Times and temperature will depend on the initial temperature of the water and how much is used. Do *not* turn on the stove.

Placing warm, inoculated milk inside a thermos bottle.

Placing the glasses of milk in an electric frying pan partially filled with warm water and set to warm.

Placing the glasses of milk on or near a radiator in the winter.

Placing the glasses of milk inside an insulated picnic box along with a bucket of hot water.

No matter what the method or means of incubation used, you will get more accurate results and possibly better results if you bring the milk up to temperature before starting incubation. You will have better control of incubation when you do this because you will not have to guess at how long it took the milk to come up to incubation temperature.

There are a number of very convenient, low-priced "home" yogurtmakers on the market today. Many large department stores and mail-order houses are offering them. The types that incorporate some kind of thermostatic control are well worth purchasing for making yogurt. You can tell it has a thermostat by listening to it. You can hear the automatic switch go on and off. The other types are little better than the top of the refrigerator or the frying pan.

All the means and devices mentioned are fine for making yogurt. Incubation need not be exact. When making culture for cheese and when making cheese, much better control is necessary if your product is to come out as you expect or desire. The home-yogurtmakers probably maintain a sufficiently stable temperature, but they cannot be adjusted to the temperature you desire, and they do not hold sufficient milk. There is little point in making a half cup of mother culture and even less in converting half a cup of yogurt to cream cheese; you'll end up with no more than a tablespoon full. For serious work you need an incubator capable of holding at least a gallon of milk. I know of no inexpensive commercial incubator of this size, but I do know how you can make your own. There are two designs, the simplex and the automatic.

The simplex is the easiest to build and the least expensive. With it you can hold the temperature of a batch of milk fairly steady for a number of hours. It is a simple "warm box" and its temperature regulation depends on the temperature of the room it is in. Since the interior of a heated house doesn't vary in temperature a great deal, the temperature of the simplex is stable enough or predictable enough to be useful.

The automatic costs more and is a little more difficult to construct. However, the automatic will hold to temperature quite well despite a twenty- to thirty-degree temperature swing in the room in which it is placed. Since it is actually a heating system, it is useful only when the room temperature is the same or lower than the temperature to which the incubator is set. It works best in an attic or basement or anyplace that is always cooler than incubation temperature.

Both the simplex and the automatic require a styrofoam picnic box, a flat-bottom porcelain socket, a length of twin-wire fixture wire, a plug, and an electric light bulb.

To make the simplex, the plug is attached to the end of

the wire. The wire is pulled through a hole in the side of the box and connected directly to the porcelain socket. A bulb is screwed into place and the socket placed in a corner of the box. A sheet of aluminum foil is hung across the box in front of the light bulb. It does not reach the bottom of the box. The foil helps distribute the heat. Without it the glass nearest the light bulb would get most of the heat.

The tickler to the simplex design is the light bulb size. I find that a 15-watt bulb is about right for 85 degrees F. inside the box when the room is about 65 degrees to 75 degrees F. The temperature can be increased by using a larger size bulb. Check the temperature by placing a quart of water in the box and measuring its temperature. Mount a standard exterior house thermometer in the room next to the warm box so you can keep track of the room temperature. Knowing the room temperature will guide you in judging the temperature inside the simplex. Very simply, if your room drops below 65 degrees F., you can be certain the inside of the incubator has also grown cooler. If the room becomes warmer, so has the interior of the incubator.

The simplex can be used with fair results if one first runs a few tests over a period of time and correlates room-to-box temperature.

The automatic requires all the parts listed for the simplex and, in addition, a "home"-type thermostat. This can be purchased in an electric supply shop for about twelve dollars. It is fairly sensitive and will hold the milk on temperature with a swing of about four degrees total. When the inside of the box, the thermostat, the lamp socket, and the batch of milk have stabilized (you speed this by bringing the milk to temperature before you place it in the box), the automatic switch will cut off about two degrees above the temperature to which it is set, and switch on about two degrees below the desired temperature. Since the average is where we want it, this is fine.

To convert the simplex to automatic, disconnect one of the wires connected to the lamp socket and connect it to one terminal on the thermostat. With a short length of insulated wire (half a piece of the fixture wire will do), connect the remaining terminal on the thermostat to the terminal on the lamp socket. A 100-watt lamp is used in place of the 15-watt lamp.

The thermostat consists of a bimetallic spiral on which a glass vial containing a bit of mercury is mounted. When it becomes cold, the spiral contracts, the vial tilts, and the mercury flows across the two wires bared inside the vial. That turns the bulb on. When warmed, the spiral expands and the vial tilts in the opposite direction. The light goes off.

To maintain the integrity of the temperature markings on the thermostat it must be mounted in a perfectly vertical position on one wall of the inside of the box. The side wall diagonally opposite the lamp is best.

If your thermostat has a top reading of 85 degrees F., and many do, this is as high as you can set your box with the "stat" in a vertical position. If you wish a higher temperature, follow this procedure: Mount the stat loosely on the wall in a vertical position. Set it to 85 degrees F. Place a quart or two of warm water (85 degrees F.) inside the box, close it, and turn it on by connecting the plug to a wall outlet. Return a few hours later and measure the temperature of the water. For ease in discussion, let us assume it is 85 degrees F. (if not, your stat is off a bit). If the lamp is on, replace the cover and wait until the light goes off. Then remove the cover and, facing the stat, slowly turn the entire device in the direction that makes the light go on. If you want the box to reach 105 degrees F., turn the stat proportionally to the angle existing between 65 degrees and 85 degrees on the stat's markings. Tighten the stat to the wall of the box and wait until she stabilizes again. Then measure the temperature. If you turn the stat just right, and you can find this position by experimentation, you will have a scale that indicates 85 degrees, when it is actually set to 105 degrees F. But remember, this will be true only when the box is perfectly level. If you place it on a pitched surface, the readings will be off again.

Be especially careful not to spill milk inside your incubator. If you do, wipe it up as quickly as possible. The incubator makes an excellent home for the very creatures we wish to avoid. When you sterilize your equipment, do not fail to do the same with the incubator. You cannot immerse the stat in bleach and water, but you can wash everything else down.

8

MAKING YOGURT AND KEFIR

If you have perused this manuscript thus far you know that milk taken from a mammal will, when kept warm, curdle of itself because of the lactic acid-producing bacteria present. You know that pasteurized milk has almost no viable lactic bacteria, and therefore it is necessary that lactic bacteria be added to pasteurized milk to make it curdle. You know there are two general sources of lactic bacteria—cultured products such as store yogurt, sour cream and buttermilk, and freeze-dried cultures that can be purchased from commercial laboratories through the mail or from local health-food shops and some grocers.

You know that incubation temperatures used for yogurt range from 70 degrees to 118 degrees F., and you know that so soon as the milk stiffens, it is yogurt and may be consumed or stored for consumption at a later date.

While all this is very useful and even interesting, what we need to know now are the specifics, for example, flavor. What is the flavor of homemade yogurt like? Can it be varied? Can it be controlled?

If you are accustomed to eating commercial yogurt purchased at the grocer's or supermarket, prepare yourself for a change. There is some similarity in the tastes of the two, but there is probably a greater difference. Flavored yogurt as presently manufactured is a kind of sweet and sour pudding with a gelatinous consistency. Homemade yogurt is stiffer; when stirred, it turns to a creamy liquid. Store yogurt remains gelatinous no matter how much you stir.

Home yogurt has a taste closer to that of milk. Store yogurt is sweeter, tastes less like milk and more like melted ice cream. Plain store yogurt contains no flavoring. It is very, very sour and its taste borders on the bitter. Sour homemade yogurt is not this acidic. Plain store yogurt has an almost cream-cheese consistency. Home yogurt, which is sour, is never as thick. Generally, when home yogurt is permitted to "ripen" all the way and develop maximum acidity the curd separates from the whey. Store yogurt rarely separates. Like homogenized milk, store yogurt is "neater" than home yogurt.

The flavor of the yogurt you make at home will depend on the milk you use and the bacterial strain or strains, assuming you do not flavor it.

Whole, skim, or any combination of whole and skim milk can be used. The skim milk may be purchased in liquid form or made by adding powder to water. If you wish, you can add sweet cream to the milk. Put enough sweet cream in and you will end up with sour cream, which of course is sweet cream that has been soured by lactic bacteria. The more milk fat used, the "sweeter" the flavor of the resultant yogurt. It will taste more like cream and less like milk.

When making yogurt, you may use any of the lactic cultures sold by labs. You need not limit yourself to the strains suggested for making yogurt. I find that some of the cheese strains result in a taste that is more pleasing to me. Generally, the yogurt strains contain *L. bulgaricus,* which can make the yogurt very sour. The cheese strains sometimes include "flavor" types or strains of bacteria. It is a matter of taste.

When you make your yogurt with lab starters, follow the procedures suggested for making and storing mother culture in Chapters 4, 5, and 6. You'll get more yogurt for your money and better-tasting yogurt, meaning yogurt more closely resembling the mother culture in taste and acidity.

If you do not want to go to the trouble of making a mother culture, and plan to inoculate a batch of milk and then use some of the resulting yogurt to inoculate the next batch of milk, expect much more rapid contamination and flavor change. The literature accompanying the lab's powdered cultures predicts a life span of about one month, meaning that you can keep making a series of glasses of yogurt for about a month before the culture weakens or is overwhelmed by outsiders. I believe that to be maximum.

You can extend the life of your yogurt series by taking care to keep the glasses covered after inoculation and by starting the succeeding batch before the first batch is all gone.

Generally, one vial or packet is used to start about a quart of milk, which is then poured into a number of containers and incubated. The labs recommend 1 to 3 teaspoons as sufficient yogurt to start a quart of milk. I find that a larger quantity insures against failure and I suggest a minimum of 2 tablespoons per quart, increasing the number of spoonfuls used with each succeeding batch of yogurt to compensate for diminishing bacterial vitality.

Some labs postulate a refrigerated life span of up to 10 days, meaning that once made, the yogurt can be used successfully as a starter if not kept more than 10 days. I find that 10 days is just about the longest one can keep lightly covered yogurt intact in the refrigerator and use it as a starter. Store it in a tightly covered, sterilized container, however, and you can keep the culture alive and well for a month or more.

It is best to inoculate the entire quantity of milk you plan to convert to yogurt and then apportion it into cups or glasses. This reduces exposure and contamination. If you are making a quart's worth of yogurt, add the starter to the milk, mix, and then divide. If you are making just a few cups, add the starter to each cup and then add the milk. With both techniques, keep the starter uncovered a minimum amount of time.

One level tablespoon equals 3 level teaspoons. If you are mixing commercial culture with just 1 glass of milk, the ratio of 2 tablespoons of culture to the quart works out to one and a fraction teaspoons to the glass. I'd use 2 just to be sure.

We follow the same procedure when using store yogurt, cultured buttermilk or sour cream as a starter. However, I suggest doubling the quantity of starter. In other words, I would use 4 tablespoons of store starter to the quart and 1 tablespoon to the standard 8-ounce glass. As yogurt and cream are thick, be certain to mix well when adding.

You can, if you wish, use store yogurt or buttermilk to

start a quart of mother culture. By doing so you will greatly reduce the quantity of preservative and sugar you would otherwise add to the yogurt you make. You may also achieve a little more stability in the activity of your culture. Once you have the quart of mother culture prepared, there will be far less change from spoonful to spoonful than if you work with a succession of glasses of yogurt.

The consistency or texture of the yogurt depends on the milk you use, how you treat it, additives, and the condition of the curd when you stop incubation and chill it.

In general, the yogurt will be somewhat more firm if you boil the skim milk you use for 30 seconds or less before inoculation. This is unnecessary with pasteurized milk, which has been heat-treated during pasteurization.

Your yogurt will be considerably firmer if you add milk powder to your milk. The labs suggest adding a minimum of 3 level tablespoons of powdered milk (the powder itself) to 1 quart of either whole milk, skim milk, or any combination of the two. If you mix your own powdered milk, just add more powder.

Some labs suggest adding 1 teaspoon of carrot juice or tomato juice to each 8-ounce glass of milk when adding the culture to thicken the resultant coagulum. I find that I can make yogurt of satisfactory taste and texture without troubling to boil the skim milk or adding milk powder or vegetable juice. I do find that the taste I like best is secured by adding about 10 percent whole milk to the skim milk.

The moment at which the incubating milk is firmest is its isoelectric point. You can, if you wish, use any of the tests described in Chapter 5 to pinpoint maximum curd firmness. However, it isn't worth the effort. Whether or not the yogurt is slightly looser or firmer is hardly noticeable when you spoon it out. The difference in taste is slight. However, if you plan to store the yogurt for any length of time, stop incubation early, and by all means, do not let the yogurt overripen. If it proceeds to separation it will be much more sour than at its isoelectric point, and if the curd separates from the whey, you lose that much milk nutrient, since most people do not drink whey, at least I don't, so this is poured off and wasted.

When the coagulum is close to its firmest condition, remove it from the heat and chill. You can eat warm yogurt, but most people prefer it cold. A few hours in the refrigerator will cool it thoroughly. Chilling firms the curd a bit and changes its flavor in the sense that cold yogurt tastes different than warm yogurt. The difference is far greater than you might imagine.

We have stated that incubation temperature ranges from 70 degrees to 118 degrees F., but what exactly should you use? If the culture packet contains instructions, follow them. If you are using store yogurt or cultured buttermilk, I suggest you choose a temperature between 86 degrees and 100 degrees F. The exact temperature is not critical, but it is important to stick with one temperature so that you will know how long incubation takes. This will save time and indicate the condition of the bacteria. Delayed coagulation will warn you of reduced bacterial activity and you will be able to take corrective steps of increasing starter quantity and eventually going on to fresh starter.

Hansen's recommends that its "yogurt" be incubated at 98 degrees to 108 degrees F. for 6 to 10 hours. Their yogurt culture is a combination of *Lactobacillus bulgaricus* and *Streptococcus thermophilus*. The same lab suggests the same temperature and time span for their "acidophilus yogurt," which is a combination of *L. bulgaricus, S. thermophilus,* and *L. acidophilus.* This mixture is supposed to have a more palatable, distinctive nutlike flavor. (The L. acidophilus has been proven capable of establishing themselves in the intestinal tract of ingesting individuals.) Note that the presence of *L. acidophilus* makes it necessary to use only skim milk with the culture. Even so, the results may be somewhat lumpy and granular.

Hansen's also offers "acidophilus milk." It is made as a yogurt, following the same temperature and time schedule. Only a single strain, *L. acidophilus,* is employed, resulting in an acid flavor. To convert the yogurt to milk, simply stir. Many people add fresh milk and fruit or fruit flavoring for a better taste.

L. acidophilus doesn't fare too well in the refrigerator. According to the lab, most of the little creatures cash in their chips after 48 hours. The lab therefore suggests that a transfer be made before the two days are over, and that after a total time lapse of two weeks, the existing culture be consumed and a fresh batch started with another packet of freeze-dried acidophilus. For best results they suggest that the skim milk, which should always be used when acidophilus is present, be boiled prior to inoculation.

Rosell Institute cultures, distributed by The International Yogurt Company, contain four species of lactic bacteria: *S. thermophilus, L. bulgaricus, L. yogurtii,* and *L. acidophilus.* The proportion is about 50 percent Streptococci and 50 percent Lactobacilli. (The address is to be found in the Appendix.) Rosell suggests its yogurt culture be incubated at 118 degrees F. At this temperature coagulation will occur in 2¾ to 4 hours.

Incidentally, if you do not like the taste of yogurt but

would still like a go at its health-giving properties, International distributes yogurt tablets. Each tablet contains a minimum of 10 million active creatures. Two a day are suggested. The tablets can be kept active for more than a year if refrigerated. The tablets contain Streptococcus thermophilus, Lactobacillus acidophilus and Lactobacillus bulgaricus.

As yogurt is known by many names—mazun, kisselo-mleko, maja, leben, nono, leben rain, dadhi, gioddu, yohurt, and yoghurt—many health-food writers have confused kefir with yogurt. Kefir is not another name for yogurt. Kefir is like yogurt in that it contains lactic bacteria which causes the milk to ferment. But it is unlike yogurt in that it also contains yeast cells, which produce alcohol and carbon dioxide. Generally, kefir will contain 1 percent lactic acid and 1 percent alcohol, but sometimes may go as high as 4 percent alcohol, which makes it more potent than the 3.5 percent beer of yesteryear.

Kefir is made in much the same way as yogurt. You start with a culture—in this case, kefir culture purchaseable at some health-food shops and from the Rosell labs for about the same price as yogurt culture. The packet is used to inoculate a quart of pasteurized milk at 70 degrees F., which is its incubation temperature. Most often, all you need do is keep it in the kitchen. The container cannot be tightly closed, since the liberated carbon dioxide gas must be permitted to escape. Incubation requires from 24 to 30 hours and is complete when the milk has curdled. The same methods and tests are used as with yogurt. The container of kefir may now be closed.

For all practical purposes you have the equal of a quart of yogurt culture on hand. The only difference is that its incubation temperature is lower and the incubating vessel must not be sealed while the milk ferments. As with yogurt culture, you can refrigerate the kefir mother culture at 40 degrees F. and use it later to start cups of kefir and successive quarts of mother culture. Or you can chill the quart of kefir you just made and prepare it, when cold, for serving. Usually the kefir is stirred, shaken or beaten into a light cream before eating.

Should you wish to make thick kefir for eating with a spoon, Rosell recommends mixing 2 glasses of whole milk with 2 glasses of evaporated milk and inoculating the mixture with 3 or 4 tablespoons of kefir culture. The mixture is poured into cups or glasses and incubated as necessary. The kefir is chilled after curdling and before serving.

As an alternative to using evaporated milk, you can add about ¾ cup of milk powder to 1 quart of whole milk, mixing it well before adding the starter.

It is interesting to note that kefir is recommended by Rosell for expectant mothers who find other food difficult to take, as well as for all others suffering from any of the stomach-associated disorders discussed in Chapter 2.

While we are on the subject of exotic foods, a few words on Kumiss, a fermented-milk drink once popular in Russia and Western Asia. The genuine article is made from unheated mare's milk. As can be imagined, Kumiss in its legitimate form has a very individual flavor and quite a kick. Mare's milk is high in lactose, and the fermenting agents contain our old friends *L. bulgaricus* and *S. lactis,* plus a generous helping of yeast. As yeast feeds on lactose, it is not surprising that the alcohol content of Kumiss goes better than 3 to 4 percent. In Siberia and places further east, Kumiss is distilled and made into a brandy. This would indicate that some Kumiss approaches the alcoholic content of wine.

There is no commercial source of Kumiss culture in this country, but even if you could buy some, who'd you get to milk the horse?

Up front somewhere, we promised a few words on making butter at home; that's all the directions needed.

To make your own butter, one chills a pint or so of sweet cream, the heavier the better, but any kind except half-and-half will do. The amount used is unimportant.

Place the cold sweet cream in a closed bottle of any kind having a large mouth and shake. At first nothing. With a little puffing you will get whipped cream. This may not want to shake very much, but persist. The whipped cream will give way to a thinner liquid with fine clusters of milk fat globules. More shaking and the clusters will gather and form one or two large lumps. At this point, stop shaking and open the bottle. Use a fork to bring the clumps together. Pour the liquid into a glass. It is real buttermilk. Place the clumps of golden butter on a plate and use your fork to press out the remaining drops of buttermilk. You now have unsalted butter. If you wish, you can work a little salt into it. That's all there is to it.

Should you want some of that hard to get, old-fashioned tub butter, add 1 tablespoon of commercial culture (the kind used for cottage cheese) to each pint of cream you plan to use, or 2 tablespoons of cultured buttermilk to each pint. Incubate the pint of cream at 86 degrees F. for four hours. Chill thoroughly. It is hard to make butter when the cream isn't cold.

Shake if that provides the exercise you want or use an

egg beater, hand or powered, until you get the milk fat to separate from the liquid and form butter.

This is a fun method of bringing home the butter, but it is not an economical way. 1 pint of whipping cream makes about ½ pound of butter or a little less.

9

MAKING CHEESE

There are some seven basic kinds of cheese that can be readily made at home. They are cream, pot, cottage, Farmer, Muenster, American, and Cheddar. The making of these cheeses is herewith described in detail along with a word on variations and some information on making several Italian cheeses. Should you wish to go further afield, you would do well to secure U.S. Department of Agriculture Handbook No. 54, *Cheese Varieties and Descriptions.* Along with semitechnical descriptions of more than four hundred different cheeses, the book gives some general manufacturing tips.

In reading Handbook No. 54, other government publications, culture and rennet manufacturer's literature, technical books on cheesemaking and when possibly talking to people engaged in cheesemaking, you may find their cheesemaking methods differ markedly from the methods present here. Or you will probably find the rennet-to-milk ratios to be different too. My methods are not the only methods, but I do believe they are the simplest and best suited to individuals like ourselves with limited experience and even less equipment. In the matter of rennet quantity, it may well be we are all suggesting the same quantity of rennet. All the tablets look pretty much alike. It is the rennet they contain that varies. So that where the U.S. Department of Agriculture's Home and Garden Bulletin No. 29 suggests ¼ tablet, their tablet may have far less rennet than the Salada tablets (and Hansen's) that I am using, since for a similar process I suggest 1/16 tablet.

In the matter of incubation temperature and associated time, many of the brochures suggest 16 to 24 hours. (With temperatures adjusted to suit.) This is fine. But for me, I find 16 hours awkward. A slightly better flavor and curd will result when using a lower temperature and a little less starter than I recommend, but I believe the increased chance of early contamination and inconvenient time span are much too high a price to pay. Hence, I strive for a 10-hour incubation period. You may prefer a longer or shorter period. If you have been paying close attention, you know how to effect the change.

Suggested cooking temperatures vary. The one rule to follow is, *lower is better* and *longer is always safer.* But curd doesn't always respond the way you would like it to, so raise the temperature as high as necessary and cook as long as necessary to secure the curd you wish.

Some of the seven cheeses can be made from milk ranging in fat content from 1 percent (skim) to 4 percent (whole). Others can only be made from skim milk. For example, if you make pot cheese from milk containing much more than 1 percent milk fat, you end up with a kind of American cheese.

To vary the fat content of the milk, simply mix whole milk with skim milk. The proportions necessary to attain various milk-fat contents are given in Chapter 3.

The fat content of your cheese depends on the fat content of the milk you use and the quantity of cheese that results from your efforts. If you make cream cheese from 4-percent milk, your cheese will not have a milk-fat content of 4 percent, but will be closer to 16 percent. Commercial cream cheese has a milk-fat content of 33 percent at a minimum. In some states it may run to 38 percent. Incidentally, homemade 16-percent milk-fat cream cheese tastes as good or better than commercial 33-percent-fat cheese.

An easy way to compute the milk-fat content of your cream cheese and all the cheeses you make is to compare the weight of the finished cheese to the weight of the milk used. The milk-fat content will be in the same proportion. For those in fourth year math, and I took math four years,

cheese-fat content : milk-fat content
:: cheese weight : milk weight.

For example, start with a gallon of milk. It weighs 8.25 pounds, but we shall use the 8; it is accurate enough. We know that most of the milk fat remains with the curd and ends up in the cheese. Therefore, if we start with 8 pounds of 4 percent milk and finish with 2 pounds of cream cheese, we have reduced the weight of the milk (it is now cheese) by four. The proportion of fat to the milk remaining has been increased four times, ergo, the fat content is 16 percent. If we only get 1 pound of cheese (and little or nothing was lost in the process), then the 8 pounds of milk has been reduced to one pound of cheese and the original 4-percent fat content has been increased proportionally eight times, to 32 percent. If this is not clear, think of it this way. There isn't any more fat; there is simply less milk. Eight pounds of milk weighs 128 ounces. If 4 percent is fat, we have a little more than 5 ounces of fat present. Make cheese and we still have the 5 ounces of fat, but the total weight (1 pound) is only 16 ounces. The percentage of fat has increased.

Since many of the steps and formulas for making the seven cheeses are similar, the significant differences will be discussed first, and then we will go on to making the individual cheeses.

Cream cheese is a high-acid, small-curd cheese, which means the inoculated milk is permitted to coagulate on its own. Usually, no rennet is added. The coagulum is usually cooked, but never stirred or washed during cooking or afterward. Instead the coagulum is drained and salted, and after chilling is ready for consumption.

Cottage cheese is also a high-acid, small-curd cheese. It differs from cream cheese in that nothing but skim milk is ever used. The curd is stirred during cooking, and may be washed at this time. Even if washed during cooking, it is always thoroughly washed after cooking, then drained and salted.

Cottage cheese may be curdled either by acid action alone or with the addition of a little rennet. The acid method produces a smaller curd than the rennet method, which produces a milder, firmer cheese.

Drained and lightly salted cottage cheese is known and consumed under a number of names: Dutch cheese,

Schmierkase, country-style, farm-style, or small-curd pot cheese and just plain cottage cheese.

To convert just plain cottage cheese to creamed cottage cheese one adds cream and mixes. It may be sweet cream, it may be sour cream, it may be cultured buttermilk (yogurt). When the cream added is sour, the entire cheese appears to be sour and "tangy." If you take the trouble to separate the curds from the cream of commercial cottage cheese and taste both individually, you will find most of the sourness lies in the cream. By comparison, the cheese itself is bland and moist. Legally, creamed cottage cheese must contain 4 percent milk fat or more to warrant the name. Commercial cheese may not have a total moisture content of more than 80 percent. Usually it is about 70 percent.

Pot cheese is like cottage cheese in that it is made only from skimmed milk. Pot cheese is sometimes called large-curd or sweet-curd cheese. In some countries it is also known as popcorn cheese, sweet-curd cottage cheese, flake-type cottage cheese, and low-acid, or rennet-type cottage cheese.

Pot cheese differs from cottage cheese in that the curd is less acid. Rennet is used to produce coagulation sometime before maximum- or high-acid levels are reached—hence the name sweet-curd. Like cottage cheese, it is stirred or mixed during cooking and like cottage cheese, the curd may be washed during cooking. In any event, this cheese is always thoroughly washed after cooking. Washing is followed by draining and salting. Like the previously mentioned cheeses, it is then ready to eat, though most people prefer it chilled.

Farmer cheese may be likened to cream cheese with less milk fat and more body, or to cottage or pot cheese with more milk fat and perhaps a little less body. You can, if you wish, shape cottage or pot cheese and call it Farmer cheese. In France, this variety was originally made on farms exactly the way cottage cheese was made and called Fromage à la Pie, Mou, Maigre, or Ferme. The pressed shape in which it is often sold in cheese shops today is reminiscent of the methods used by French farmers, who would place the curds in a cloth sleeve and place a weight on it to draw out the whey.

Farmer cheese can be made of skim milk, whole milk, or a mixture of both. I think the use of whole milk, alone or with very little skim milk in the mixture, makes for better flavor. Coagulation can be by acid alone or acid plus rennet. In the latter case, rennet quantity is limited to permit the curd to become quite acidic, almost as acidic as if no rennet were used. The curd is mixed during cooking. Generally it is washed after cooking, drained, salted, and pressed very lightly. The cheese may be eaten fresh or pressed more firmly and aged.

American cheese technically includes the Cheddars, Colby, Monterey Jack, and others. But the cheese we make will taste somewhat like the American we purchase in the supermarket, although not exactly, since theirs is processed.

American is made of "ripened" milk that is coagulated by rennet. At the time of coagulation the curd is never as acidic as any of the fresh or white cheeses we have just discussed. The cut curd is mixed during cooking, washed, drained, salted, and pressed. Generally it is aged somewhat before consumption. Sharp American is made the same way but the milk is permitted to ripen a bit longer (become more acid) before coagulation. The sharp taste is developed by curing—letting the cheese age for six months or more.

Cheddar begins as an American cheese. The milk is permitted to ripen a bit longer. The curd is cut into smaller pieces, cooked a little longer, and then drained. When draining is nearly complete, the curd is salted and returned to the warm pot where cooking continues until the curds slump into one piece, whereupon the single piece is cut into small pieces again, washed, drained, salted, and pressed very hard. The purpose of the double cooking and the extra-hard pressing is to remove more whey than is removed from American cheese. Cheddar is harder than American cheese. It can be eaten fresh, but is best when cured, the longer the better. The best Cheddar may be three years old.

The Muenster I like resembles a semisoft, springy, sour type of American. My favorite is by no means the only variation; there must be fifty different Muensters for sale in the United States alone. It is named after the town of Munster in the Vosges Mountains of western Germany, as you can see, it has traveled considerably. Gerardmer, made across the border in France, is purportedly a similar cheese. So if you wish to upstage your friends, tell them you are making Gerardmer.

Muenster tastes best when made with whole milk, but you can use about 25 percent skim without altering the flavor too much. The milk is allowed to ripen for about as long as the milk used for Cheddar. The curd is cut in very large pieces and permitted to soak at a slightly elevated temperature for two hours. Then it is stirred and cooked in the conventional manner. The soaking produces the moist, springy texture. Following cooking it is drained, washed, pressed lightly after salting. It may be eaten ripe or cured for several months.

In the process of making cheese you may be making quantities of skim milk. Rather than measuring both powder and water, simply add water to the requisite quantity of powder until you have the quantity of milk you want. The basic quantities are as follows:

Powder	To Make
1-1/3 cups + water	1 quart
2-2/3 cups + water	2 quarts
4 cups + water	3 quarts
5-1/3 cups + water	1 gallon

I've measured my cheese pot off with cups of water to locate the two-quart and four-quart marks. At these levels I've enscribed some marks with an ice pick. When I want a gallon of powdered milk, I dump 5-1/3 cups of powder into the pot and add water slowly, mixing as I go, until I reach the gallon mark.

When I plan on adding cold milk (it's cold from the refrigerator), I start with hot water when mixing the reconstituted skim milk. Then the cold milk brings the temperature down to about where I want it. When it's going to be all skim, I adjust the water tap to get the 86 degrees F. I plan to use for incubation. It is a lot easier to mix the powder with warm water than with cold, and you save on the time otherwise needed to warm the milk up. There is nothing wrong with using hot water from the tap.

When you mix powder and water, mix slowly so as not to make bubbles. If they do appear, skim them off with a spoon—you can mix forever without making them go away. And be certain all the powder is dissolved. Lumps that remain on the bottom of the pot will remain lumps right through the processes and into the cheese.

As cream cheesemaking is an almost infallible process, let us start with it.

You can use store-starter; buttermilk, yogurt, etc., but you will have better-tasting cheese if you inoculate your milk with a commercial culture developed especially for cream cheese. See the Appendix for suggested commercial cultures.

As cream cheese is the most economical cheese to make—less whey is lost than with any other type of cheese—you will probably want to start with less than a gallon of milk. One-half gallon of milk should make about a pound of cheese.

Start by adding ¼ cup of commercial starter to ½ gallon of milk. Alternately, you can use ½ cup cultured buttermilk or yogurt. Incubate at 86 degrees F. for about 10 hours, or until the milk curdles and you approach its isoelectric point. (We discussed this in Chapter 5, "Coagulating.") You now have two possible courses of action open to you. You can gently transfer the curd to a cloth bag made very easily from a square of well-washed muslin, picking it up by the four corners, and then hanging the bag up in a cool place with a draining rack underneath. Or you can spread the same cloth over the inside of a colander and stand the colander over a pot, which collects the drip. On a hot day, you can place the colander and pot inside the refrigerator.

When the curd has stopped draining, it has probably reached the desired moisture content. There is no harm in peeking. The presence of moisture on the exterior of the cloth is a false indication of the amount of moisture in the cheese. There is always more water on the cloth, because it is dripping downward. Flavor cheese by mixing in about 1 level teaspoon of fine salt.

Bear in mind that since the cheese contains a considerable quantity of whey, there are microbes at work. So chill the cheese as soon as you have salted it, or it will grow more sour.

If you want a cheese that is firmer, but not dry, follow the same procedure. However, when the curd reaches its isoelectric point, cut it into ½-inch cubes using the technique shown in the accompanying illustration. After cutting, the curd is permitted to sit for 20 to 30 minutes at incubation temperature. The curd will shrink somewhat—you will see the "cut" marks grow wider—and free whey will appear. Place the cheese pot inside the outer water-filled pot. Put the assembly of pots and water on the stove and slowly raise the temperature of the curd.

Cutting the Curd. You need a long, sharp knife, long enough to reach diagonally all the way across your pot. Start by cutting parallel lines—as far apart as the desired cube size—in one direction. Then cut across the first set of lines. Next cut at an angle, as shown, from both sides. You won't make evenly sized cubes, but you can cut the big ones down when they appear while mixing.

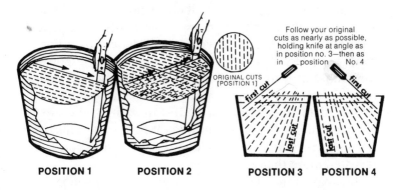

Follow your original cuts as nearly as possible, holding knife at angle as in position no. 3—then as in position No. 4

ORIGINAL CUTS [POSITION 1]

first cut

last cut

POSITION 1   POSITION 2   POSITION 3   POSITION 4

I suggest you try the noncook method first. If that doesn't produce the consistency you want, try the second method, stopping at the point where you have let the cut curd soak at incubation temperature. If this still doesn't produce the consistency you desire, have a third go at it, and bring the temperature slowly up to about 95 degrees F., no more. Do not mix, as you do not want to damage the curd. Adjust the heat so that at least 30 minutes transpire before the curd temperature, as measured inside the inner pot, reaches 95 degrees F. Remember, the more you cook, the more cheese is lost to the whey. I use no more heat and time than are necessary to reduce the cubes slightly.

When cooking is finished, repeat the drain operation described previously, salt, and enjoy.

After cream cheese, American is the variety most easily made at home. There are, as we stated, two kinds. Both are made the same way, differing only in the degree of acidity and curing. A sharp American cheese before aging is a mild American that is slightly more sour to the taste. The "sharp" flavor can only be produced by aging, the longer the better.

Since you will only get about a pound of American from a gallon of milk, and since the curds of American cheese must be mixed, I would not advise attempting to work with less than 1 gallon of milk or using a pot that can't hold at least 1½ gallons of milk. You will of course need an outer pot to make a double-boiler arrangement.

Inoculate the gallon of milk with either ½ cup of commercial starter or 1 cup of cultured buttermilk. The commercial starter is preferred for reasons probably repeated more than once.

Incubate for 2 hours at 86 degrees F. Remember, the

milk must be at incubation temperature at the start of the countdown. Now dissolve ¼ Hansen's rennet tablet, or 2½ Salada tablets, in ¼ glass of cold water. Make certain the rennet is thoroughly dissolved. Add the rennet to the milk, mixing thoroughly. Note the time the rennet was added. Note when coagulation begins. Follow the Renner formula—2½ times the length of time it takes for coagulation to start. Or use any of the other tests suggested for determining the isoelectric point, the moment when the curd is best to cut. Coagulation should occur about 25 to 35 minutes after the rennet has been added. If it occurs faster, cut the quantity of rennet you are using (next time, spill out some of the dissolved rennet).

Cut the curd into ½-inch cubes. Stand back and watch the lines appear. Wait 30 minutes, then begin applying more heat and raising the temperature above the original 86 degrees F. If your cheese pot has been in your incubator up until now, the time has come to put it into the outer pot and put both on the stove top.

The temperature of the curd should be raised slowly. This is called cooking. As the curd grows warmer it shrinks, expelling whey. At the same time it becomes proportionately stronger and firmer. American cheese is moderately moist—not as moist as Muenster and not as dry as Cheddar—so we have cut the curd into moderate-sized pieces. Muenster, moist for a cheese of this general type, is cut into ¾-inch cubes. Cheddar is cut into ¼-inch cubes.

The exact rate at which the temperature of the curd is raised is unimportant, but it is very important that it takes at least 30 minutes or longer to get to 104 degrees F. Curd is a comparatively poor conductor of heat. When the temperature of the whey in which the cubes are floating is increased, the outside of the cubes get warmer first, the inside last. If the temperature comes up too rapidly, the outside of the cube shrinks—you can actually see the cubes turn almost into ball shapes—and further insulate the inside of the cube. The outside of a rounded cube will be tough, leathery and skinlike. The inside will be mush. You cannot make cheese from mush.

As curd is a poor conductor of heat, the cubes near the bottom and sides of the pot grow warmer first, the cubes in the middle last. Therefore you must begin mixing so soon as the temperature rises appreciably. At first the cubes will occupy most of the space and there will not be sufficient clearance for actual mixing. Use a spoon or your hand to carefully remove cubes from the center of the pot and place them near the edges. Do not attempt to insert your spoon and mix all the cubes around like stew. They are too soft. You will crush them. Remember, every crushed or squished piece of curd is lost. It becomes liquid and passes through the straining cloth or colander.

As the pieces of curd shrink, more and more whey appears in the pot, giving you more room to mix. When you can, use your spoon or your washed hand to mix. Again, do so very slowly and carefully. When you put your hand inside you will notice the temperature differential; it is cooler in the center of the pot, so make sure to move more pieces of curd to the side of the pot, to expose them to the heat.

As you mix you will see pieces of curd that are much larger than the rest. Cut them into smaller pieces. The reason for the smaller size is that all the other pieces—I call them cubes, but few will actually be perfect cubes—have already shrunk a bit and you want all the curd to be cooked evenly.

Generally, when you permit the cut curd to soak a while before increasing the temperature and mixing, the curds do not stick to each other. But if they do, hack them into pieces. Do not trouble about their original shapes, just hack away.

You need not mix constantly, but you are advised to stay with the pot the first few times until you learn to judge the condition of the curds, whether or not they are going to stick and whether or not the temperature is coming up too fast.

If the curds start to round off (don't mistake breaking for rounding), reduce the heat. Check the temperature of the water in the outer pot. If it is more than a few degrees above the temperature of the inner pot, separate the pots. This will slow down and eventually stop the cooking process.

Raising the temperature of the cheese pot and its contents ½ degree per minute or so appears to be very difficult, and it is if you work that way. The easy approach is to turn your stove to low and just wait for it to come up. If you have an electric stove like mine, the "warm" button is just right. With a gas stove you will have to experiment to find the flame that gives the increase you want. Once you have found it, a thermal check every now and again will suffice.

We have specified 104 degrees F. as our target temperature. This is a good, moderate temperature to work for, but is little more than a guide. You have got to keep your eye on the curd and work with the temperature to suit the response of your curd, and this will vary from time to time.

Our goal is a curd as firm and moist at its center as it is at its surface. We are seeking curds that respond to the passage of a knife much like putty. We want curds that do not stick together when you compress a handful and that spring lightly apart when released.

If you bring the heat up slowly enough you will never be troubled with curds that squish when you try to cut them. If you mix often enough you will not be troubled by curds that mat together on the bottom and form one mass. If you use the edge of your spoon or a knife to cut a test curd every once in a while as you mix, you can keep close tabs on the state of the curds.

Knowing just when the cubes are ready comes with experience. You can judge them better if you remove a few and cool them in cold water. Let a few minutes pass; it takes time for the heat to escape. Bear in mind that the curd stiffens when cold and stiffens a bit more when it dries. As a general guide, I suggest you stop cooking a little earlier than you believe correct, at least the first few times you make cheese.

Cutting and cooking. The drawings are exact replicas of the curd size when making various types of cheese, assuming you manage to cut a number of them into perfect cubes, which is unlikely. But the drawings furnish a general guide.

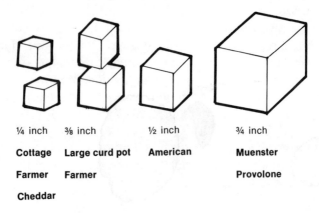

¼ inch	⅜ inch	½ inch	¾ inch
Cottage	Large curd pot	American	Muenster
Farmer	Farmer		Provolone
Cheddar			

Another general point. The more fat in the milk, the more sensitive the curd is to heat. You need to cook high-fat-content milk more slowly, that is raise the temperature more slowly than skim milk.

As the temperature of the curd rises, it becomes more solid, less soft. Eventually, it will reach the firm-bodied condition you are seeking. This may occur before the temperature reaches 104 degrees F. If so, fine. There is no reason to cook to any temperature or for any period of time if you have achieved the results you want. If the curd is not ready at about 100 degrees F., cut the heat and let the pot drift. It will reach 104 degrees F. and higher without additional external heat. Should it appear to be drifting about 104 degrees F., remove the inner pot to hold the temperature down. You don't want to lower it, but you don't want it to go up either. A few degrees one way or another won't matter, but don't let it run away.

Hold the curd at 104 degrees F., mixing and testing every 15 minutes or so, for at least an hour. If you still haven't coaxed the curds into the condition you want, bring the temperature slowly higher. But don't lose patience and turn the heat up if you do not see immediate results at 104 degrees F.

Generally, 115 degrees to 120 degrees F. should suffice for American cheese even if you are using a mix that is half whole milk and half skim milk. If the curd still isn't firm enough, let it soak a while at this temperature before going higher. Usually the need for high cooking temperature is brought on by rapid early temperature rise. A skin has formed on the cubes, insulating the inside. Increasing the temperature merely firms the skin. The long heat soak is the better solution.

Should you go for American cheese several times and still find the curds unresponsive and soft even at high cooking temperature, try adding milk powder to the milk. I prefer the texture without the extra powder, but you can add up to 2/3 cup of powder to a gallon of milk, whole or skim, without making the resultant cheese overly solid. The powder is added and thoroughly mixed before the culture is added.

It may appear at first evaluation that our mild American is very mild indeed. The short wait before adding the rennet is deceiving. Actually, incubation proceeds far longer than the 2 hours would indicate. There is the wait until the curd is ready for cooking, and this may add 1½ hours. Following, the curd is cooked for at least 1 hour. Since cooking is conducted at an elevated temperature, incubation is accelerated for most strains of bacteria—at least until 110 degrees F. or more is reached. Thus, mild American is incubated for a minimum of 4½ hours' actual time, and probably closer to 6 hours if the effects of higher temperature are included.

When cooking is complete the curds are placed in a cloth-lined colander and lightly washed in lukewarm water at a temperature of about 100 degrees F. The curd is encouraged to drain by rolling it in the cloth. Afterward it is salted. Use about 1 tablespoon of fine salt to the curds resulting from 1 gallon of milk.

Salting is a bit tricky. If you wait until the curds are completely drained, whatever salt you add remains with the cheese. However, by that time the curds have grown cold and become difficult to press into shape; they lose their plasticity. I salt before draining is complete. Then I taste as I add the curds to the hoop and add salt as necessary. Pressing and curing are discussed in Chapter 12.

Mild American can be eaten fresh from the hoop or aged a bit. Mild American can be made "sharp" by aging alone, however, a better taste will result if you start with a more acidic cheese.

Sharp American and other cheeses are sometimes colored. The usual color is orange, though any of the food colors can be used. The common coloring material is annatto and can be purchased in tablet form from any cheesemaking supply house. It is a very powerful coloring agent and a little goes a long way. A small fraction of a tablet will color a pound or two of cheese. There are two precautions pertaining to coloring: It must always be mixed into the milk well in advance of adding the rennet; and the tablets are very hard so the piece you chip off should be soaked in cold water for half an hour prior to using. If you don't, you may find small bright flecks of orange in your cheese.

You can increase the acid present in your American cheese simply by waiting three hours instead of two before adding the ¼ tablet of Hansen's rennet. You will get more than a one-third increase in acidity because of the nature of bacterial activity; probably double the acid level. I'd try the mild American first. It may be sour enough for your taste, and if it tastes sour it probably has enough acid to respond satisfactorily to curing.

Should you want a still more acidic American cheese, it is safer to follow the delayed-rennet procedure, rather than extend the three-hour waiting period. In the delayed procedure we use far less rennet and add it later. In this case, we inoculate the milk as before and wait four hours, then add 1½ Salada rennet tablets (1/8 Hansen's tablet). When the curd is ready, cut and cook as before.

Muenster may be made from whole milk or a

combination of whole and skim, but I find the Muenster poor if more than about 25 percent skim milk is used in the mixture.

Again we begin with the same starter-to-milk ratio; ½ cup commercial starter or 1 cup buttermilk to 1 gallon of milk. As with the American, you can "stiffen" the curd by using more powder, but I would be chary and would hold it down to ½ cup maximum to 1 gallon of milk. We use the same 86 degrees F. incubation temperature and add ¼ Hansen's rennet tablet or 2½ Salada tablets after 3 hours. Alternately, you can use the delayed system: 1½ Salada tablets 4 hours after incubation is initiated.

When the curd reaches its isoelectric point, we cut it into ¾-inch cubes, and then raise the temperature of the curd to 90 degrees F. and let the cut curd or cubes soak at this temperature for 2 hours. Then we start the temperature upward again very, very slowly and cook the mix in the conventional manner, making sure to raise the temperature very gradually.

Try not to go above 104 degrees F. And you can try by simply cutting the heat and letting the curds soak at this temperature for another hour or so before you increase the heat. Remember, you want a large, soft, moist curd; the only way to get it is to give the heat plenty of time to penetrate the large cubes.

When ready, the curd is drained, washed in cool water—not icy—salted, and hooped. Use about 1¼ tablespoons of fine salt and about 2 tablespoons caraway seed if desired. Hold the curds in the colander until they are cool, but not cold. Muenster has small mechanical openings resulting from curds that are not pressed completely into one mass.

Muenster itself is usually not colored, though its

outer rind often is. You can do this by mixing a little annatto with a little water in a flat dish and rolling the cheese, after it has been removed from the hoop, in the orange water.

Muenster may be enjoyed fresh or slightly aged (about three or four months). Since Muenster is a very moist cheese, it is more attractive to mold than American or Cheddar. To stave off their attacks—which result in a slippery surface and an odor—rub the surface down with coarse salt if you plan to age the cheese.

We begin the making of Cheddar exactly as we begin the making of sharp American; the same starter-milk ratio, the same incubation temperature, and we add the ¼ Hansen's rennet tablet 3½ hours after start of incubation. We can use whole milk or a half-whole and half-skim mixture. The use of whole milk yields a better taste, to me anyway. Using a proportion of 50 percent skim milk cuts cost and produces a harder cheese. For a very firm cheese, add up to 2/3 cup extra milk powder.

As with American and Muenster, we cut the curd at the isoelectric point, but we cut it into ¼-inch cubes. We want a very firm end product. We wait 30 minutes for initial shrinkage and then begin our cooking and mixing process. Again, we try to get the job done without going above 104 degrees F., and again we take at least 30 minutes to bring the temperature from 86 degrees F. to 104 degrees F. and even longer. But if an hour at 104 degrees F. doesn't do the job, we go higher.

When the curds are a little softer than we would like them to be for making American cheese, we gently empty the curds into a colander, thus ridding ourselves of the whey. Next we return the drained curd to the dry pot and spread two heaping tablespoons of coarse salt over the cubes and mix gently. The cover is replaced on the pot and the pot is returned to its position within the outer pot. The heat is shut off and the water temperature is measured. We want to cook our dry and salted curd at 90 degrees to 100 degrees F. To do so the water should be at a temperature of about 95 degrees to 105 degrees F., no higher. If higher, add cold water to the outer pot.

The temperature of the curds is held within this range and the curds are examined every 15 minutes or so. When the curds have slumped into a single mass, we have a go at it with our knife and hack it into 1-inch or so pieces. More whey is released. This is poured off. At this time the curd should be moderately firm and, if pulled apart, should tear like white meat from a chicken. If you touch a hot iron to the curd, you should be able to draw a ½- to 1-inch string, indicating that it is sufficiently acidic. (I just taste it.) In any event, the curd is now rinsed in luke-warm water, drained, salted again (most of the salt ran off with the whey), hooped, and pressed.

I suggest you make careful mental note of the taste of the curd after its second cooking and the taste and texture of the final product. Should you want a harder cheese, extend the cooking period the next time round. The same goes for the salt. Cheddar contains proportionately the most salt of all the cheeses we are discussing. Incidentally, your finished cheese will run from ½ to ¾ pound to the gallon of milk.

The business of cutting the curd mass and cooking it a second time is called Cheddaring. Whether the term was originally applied only to the second cutting of the curd or the second cooking or the entire operation, I have never been able to find out. All the books give a different version.

Good Cheddar is crumbly, and not rubbery. If it is

rubbery, you let the temperature go too high or get up there too quickly. Good Cheddar is quite sour when it goes into the hoop; 0.5 percent acid is about right.

Cheddar can be eaten fresh. If you have just made your first batch it is probably just as well: no point in waiting three years to learn you left out the salt or overcooked the curd.

And now on to delicious, delicate, and more difficult to make, cottage cheese. We have two methods, the all-acid method and the simultaneous-rennet method.

Cottage cheese is always made from skim milk alone, and I suggest adding 2/3 cup of extra milk powder to your gallon of milk. It will make for a firmer curd, which will be easier to handle. Later, if you find the texture too solid, you can reduce or eliminate the extra milk powder.

We start with our standard mixture: ½ cup of commercial starter or 1 cup of cultured buttermilk and 1 gallon of milk. We incubate at 86 degrees F. and let her go to coagulation and the isoelectric point. The curd is then cut into ¼-inch pieces. Let's hold it here and go the other route.

With the rennet method, we start with the same ratio of culture to milk and the same incubation temperature. This done, we remove ½ cup of inoculated milk for our acid-coagulation (AC) test. Now we add 1/16 Salada tablet to our near-gallon of milk, and nothing to the test sample. The near-gallon and the sample are both placed in the incubator. Nine hours or so later we check the sample. The main batch of milk would have long curdled. If the sample shows the onset of coagulation or full coagulation, the main batch is ready to be cut into ¼-inch pieces. If the sample is not coagulated, we wait until it is before attacking the near-gallon of curdled milk.

Whether your milk has been coagulated entirely by

acid, or by acid and rennet, 30 minutes or so are permitted to pass while the cut curd does its preliminary shrinkage act. We now commence cooking and mixing. Again we raise the temperature very slowly. (Since there is very little milk fat present, we can go a hair's breadth faster.) Again we permit 30 minutes or more to pass before we reach 104 degrees F.

You will find the curd very, very delicate. This is the only reason that making cottage cheese and the other fresh or white cheeses is difficult. The curd must be mixed slowly and gently. Remember, every curd you squish is lost. It becomes liquid and part of the whey. When you reach 104 degrees F., shut off the stove and let her drift a while. Wait another 30 minutes, mixing as gently as you can, then turn the heat on again and gradually bring the temperature up to 115 degrees F.

As the curds heat up they will shrink and become firmer. Test them by the means suggested previously—cutting, tasting, pulling apart. But be certain that you chill the test curds before you make your evaluation. Use ice water and wait at least five minutes to be sure the curd samples are cold throughout. Also, remember that the curds will be firmer when they have drained.

If you are up to 115 degrees F., have cooked for 30 minutes or more and still haven't been able to "firm up" the curd, remove as much whey as you can without damaging or losing the curds and replace the whey with clean hot water at the same temperature. Continue cooking. With some stubborn curds you may have to go to 135 or even 150 degrees F. to make them firm.

When cooking is done, rinse the curd in lukewarm water by adding water to the pot, letting the stream hit a

148

spoon and splash around. I believe this damages fewer curds than dumping the hot and still-soft pieces in the colander.

Cottage cheese is a well-washed, moist cheese, so use a lot of water, gradually lowering its temperature until the water is as cold as it will run from your tap. The curd will be stiffer now and you can gently place it into the colander for draining and salting. I find about 1 level teaspoon of fine salt does it for me.

Creamed cottage cheese begins life the same way. Creaming is done after the curds have been chilled, drained, and salted. The process is simple. Just add cream to the curds.

You can use any kind of cream you wish, sweet or sour. Generally, a "thin" sour cream is used. You can make this cream by adding and mixing whole milk with store sour cream or you can "sour" a little thinned sweet cream. Simply add as much whole milk as you wish to sweet cream, add some starter, and incubate until you have a coagulum. This is stirred to a cream consistency. Use the same ratio of starter to milk as you used for standard yogurt. For a lower calorie count, use whole-milk yogurt to cream your cottage cheese.

Pot cheese begins with skim milk and our standard starter-to-milk ratio; ½ cup commercial starter to 1 gallon of milk. For a firmer curd, as with the cottage cheese, up to 2/3 cup additional powder can be used in the milk. But be certain to use skim milk or you will end up with a kind of American cheese curd.

The milk is inoculated and incubated at 86 degrees F. Five hours later, 1/8 Salada rennet tablet is added. When the milk curdles and reaches its isoelectric point, it is cut into 3/8-inch cubes and cooked the same way as small-curd, high-acid cottage cheese curds. That is to say, if the curds cannot be made satisfactorily friable and firm after an hour of cooking at 115 degrees F., reduce the acid level by replacing the whey with hot water of the same temperature. The AC test is not used because the curd is cut in a slightly less acidic condition than that in which the small-curd is cut. Pot cheese is not allowed to go all the way to an acid level that would produce coagulation. This is why it is called sweet curd; it is not as sour.

If you want even less acid in the final cheese, use a bit more rennet and add it earlier. If you want more acid, add less rennet and add it later.

The pot cheese curds are well washed after cooking. Again, we start with water near the temperature of the curds and we gradually use colder water until the curds are cool. A teaspoon of fine salt added to the results of a gallon of milk, which will range from 1 to 2 pounds, should be about right. The cheese is eaten fresh. It may be creamed, but usually is not.

Farmer cheese can be made by acid coagulation or by the simultaneous or delayed-rennet method. Whole milk or whole milk plus a percentage of skim milk is used. Generally no less than 50 percent whole milk is used. If a firmer cheese is wanted, and this is usual when the cheese is to be aged, additional milk powder is added in quantities of up to 2/3 cup powder per gallon of milk.

The starter-to-milk ratio is the same; ½ cup commercial starter to 1 cup cultured buttermilk to 1 gallon of milk. Incubation is at 86 degrees F. If you are going the acid-coagulation route, just wait for coagulation and the isoelectric point. The later will occur between 10 and 12 hours after the start of incubation. For a slightly firmer cheese, use the simultaneous-rennet method. Add 1/16

Salada rennet tablet after removing ½ cup of milk for the AC test. Cut the curd into ¼-inch pieces when the test milk has coagulated. If you wish less acidic cheese, use the delayed-rennet method. Start as before but add 1/8 Salada rennet tablet 5 hours after start of incubation. Cut into 3/8-inch pieces for a softer cheese.

Cooking proceeds the same way suggested for cottage cheese. The only difference is that the curd is ready somewhat sooner, meaning Farmer cheese curd may be a bit softer.

When ready, the curd is washed in lukewarm water, but not chilled. Instead it is drained and salted. One teaspoon of fine salt is about enough for the cheese resulting from a gallon of milk. The salted curd is then shaped.

You can roll it up in a layer of cloth and then flatten the cloth to make a sleeve, or you can hoop it. In any event, if the cheese is to be eaten fresh, it is merely formed into a shape. If the Farmer cheese is to be aged, it is pressed with a moderate amount of pressure. Generally, a little more salt is added when the cheese is to be aged.

Now for some Italian cheeses. We will start with Provolone, or a cheese that will be a little like it, anyway. This is a very mild soft cheese, as we are going to make it. No starter is used. Instead, we use very fresh, unripened milk, heated to 86 degrees F. We add 1 Hansen's rennet tablet, dissolved in ¼ glass of cold water, to 1 gallon of whole milk. Coagulation should take place in about 40 minutes. If sooner, use less rennet the second time around. After the curd reaches its isoelectric point, and you can find this by the Alth droopy spoon method, or the clean-break method, or the Renner formula, it is cut into ¾-inch pieces. The temperature is then slowly raised to 125 degrees F. or a little higher, if your hands can take it. I say hands because instead of mixing in the conventional manner, you insert both hands and knead the curd pieces together into one firm lump.

Remove the curds from the whey but do not discard the whey. You will use it later. Place the curd mass in a cloth bag (a folded cloth will do), squeeze the bag to shape the curds and remove some of the whey. You can make any shape you wish, incidentally. Now return the shaped curds to the hot whey, leaving the curd lump in the cloth bag. Now the temperature of the whey is brought close to boiling, but do not let it boil. You can probably do this most efficiently by removing the pot of whey from its water bucket and placing it directly on the fire. When near boiling, the heat is shut off and the curd permitted to remain in the whey until it is cold. Then the cheese is removed and drained for 24 hours. It is now soft, palatable, and ready to eat.

We can make a grating cheese by following the same procedure, but instead of eating the drained cheese, we wait until its surface is relatively dry; this will take a few days of standing in a cool, dry room. The surface of the cheese is briskly rubbed down with fine salt and kept cool for 3 to 4 days. Next it is placed in a bucket or bottle filled with brine for another 4 days. To make brine, add as much salt to water as can be dissolved. After the brine bath, the cheese is removed and air-dried after wiping with a cloth. For the next four to six months the cheese is turned over every week or so and given a rubdown with salt. If mold appears on the surface of your cheese, rub it off with salt. In six months your cheese should be as hard as a rock. It can then be grated.

Ricotta is a whey cheese, and you can make it from the whey that remains after you have made your other cheeses. You will need at least a gallon. To collect this quantity, store your whey in the refrigerator until you have enough.

We work without the double boiler. The first step consists of heating the whey until a layer of cream appears on top. When this happens, three pints of fresh, whole milk are added and the temperature of the mixture is increased until it nearly boils—but it should not be permitted to actually boil. You will see small curds rise to the top of the liquid and move away from the sides of the pot. At this time add a little less than ½ cup of strong vinegar and stir vigorously, while keeping the temperature up. Curd will rise to the surface. Skim it off and transfer it to a hoop or a cloth-lined colander for draining. When no more curds appear, you have them all. Shut off the heat and discard the liquid.

In eight or nine hours the curds will have drained sufficiently. Add salt to taste and enjoy. The Ricotta you make this way will be very sweet and soft. Don't expect to get very much from a gallon of whey.

If you make the variation of Provolone just described, you can do the Ricotta bit when you remove the curds from the hot whey and place them in a hoop or muslin bag for shaping. Forget the Provolone; increase the temperature of the whey until the cream forms on top, then add the whole milk and continue until you have removed all the Ricotta curds that show. This done, you can return the Provolone to the whey and let both cool down together.

So far we have run on as if there is never a mistake made, or at the most, limited ourself to a few casual words. Our cheeses will be defective from time to time. Sometimes, the fault will lie with the cheesemaker, sometimes with the ingredients. Here are some more common difficulties.

Too sour cheese may be the result of using milk that is not fresh, too much starter, overactive starter, or failure to remove most or all of the whey from the cheese.

Very, very sour cheese is generally caused by using *L. bulgaricus* as the sole starter or using this strain in a combination of strains but incubating at so high a temperature or for so long that *L. bulgaricus* predominates.

A bitter flavor can be caused by overaged milk and by starter contaminated with wild yeast.

A light but still noticeable unpalatable flavor and odor, present while the main flavor of the cheese may be excellent, can be caused by partially contaminated starter.

Sweetness or fruitlike flavor can be caused by contamination in the milk, equipment, or the starter. Generally, it is yeast cells causing the trouble.

Holes in the cheese may be caused by letting the curds get cold before hooping, or by lack of sufficient pressure or pressing time.

A smell associated with the surface of the cheese alone can be caused by unwashed hoops and cloths. Whey is high in sugar and when the sugar dries in an invisible layer on the equipment, it attracts bacteria. Always wash the hoops and followers even though they are dry to the touch and appear to be immaculate.

Whey on the surface of the cheese after pressing is generally a result of insufficient washing and draining followed by low-pressure shaping. The whey was trapped in pockets within the cheese and leaked out later.

Stretchy, rubbery texture usually results from too high a cooking temperature, too much rennet, or both.

If cheese tastes flat and pasty after aging, there probably was insufficient acid in the curd when it was pressed. Acid is necessary for proper curing.

If cheese has a poor taste, too little starter or contaminated starter was used.

When cheese has small soft spots and hard spots, the curd was improperly cooked. Some of the cubes were pressed while wet in the center, with hard and leather-like surfaces.

If consistency is too soft and cheese has no body, curd was cut too soon, removed from the pot too soon. Generally, pressing with more weight will not cure this condition because the curd has been broken and has no body.

All defects in cheese flavor and body are increased by improper curing. When the cheese is stored for aging at a temperature above 55 degrees F., flavor defects are intensified. If you do not have a cool place for aging your cheeses, consider the vegetable drawer in your refrigerator.

10

YOGURT AND KEFIR FORMULAS

In Chapter 8 we discussed the basics of making yogurt and kefir. For convenience the basic formulas are repeated here. Variations follow.

All the formulas given are for making 1 quart, and the ratio of starter to milk is the same as discussed in Chapter 8. When using commercial culture, we use 2 tablespoons per quart. When using store culture (buttermilk, etc.) we use 4 tablespoons per quart. (Four tablespoons equals ¼ standard cup.) When making a standard 8-ounce glass of yogurt we use 2 teaspoons of commercial starter per glass, though this is a little more than two tablespoons per quart. With store culture, we use 1 tablespoon per glass.

The ratios suggested for making yogurt are the same as those suggested for making cheese. This helps to simplify things. Coagulation should occur with the passage of the same length of time, using the same culture, when making yogurt as when making cheese.

REGULAR YOGURT

STORE STARTER

4 tablespoons culture
1 quart milk—whole or skim

Incubate at 86 degrees F., 10 to 14 hours.

HANSEN'S YOGURT

2 tablespoons starter
1 quart milk—whole or skim

Incubate at 98 degrees to 108 degrees F., 6 to 10 hours.

HANSEN'S ACIDOPHILUS YOGURT

2 tablespoons culture
1 quart skim milk, preferably boiled for 1 minute

Incubate at 98 degrees to 108 degrees F., 6 to 10 hours.

HANSEN'S ACIDOPHILUS MILK

2 tablespoons culture
1 quart skim milk, preferably boiled for 1 minute

Incubate at 98 degrees to 108 degrees F., 6 to 10 hours.

ROSELL YOGURT

2 tablespoons culture
1 quart milk—whole or skim

Incubate at 110 degrees to 115 degrees F., 3 to 4 hours.

ROSELL KEFIR (liquid)

2 tablespoons culture
1 quart milk—whole or skim

Incubate at 70 degrees F., 24 to 30 hours. When coagulated, stir until creamlike.

ROSELL KEFIR (solid)

2 tablespoons culture
½ quart whole milk, plus ½ quart evaporated milk

Incubate at 70 degrees F., 24 to 30 hours. Alternately, add 2/3 cup milk powder to 1 quart whole milk.

GENERAL DATA

Boil the reconstituted powdered milk 1 minute for a firmer curd.

Add 1 to 3 tablespoons of milk powder to each quart of milk for a finer curd.

Add 1 to 3 tablespoons of carrot or tomato juice to each quart of milk for a firmer curd.

For a smoother flavor when using skim milk alone, add about 10 percent whole milk to the skim milk.

For a very sweet, creamy yogurt, add ¼ cup light sweet cream to the quart of whole milk.

TO FLAVOR YOGURT

You have the option of adding flavor before the milk has coagulated or afterward. It is generally better to add it afterward. Prior adding can adversely affect the coagulum. The curd may separate from the whey, coagulation may be delayed and in some cases prevented. When such difficulties arise, double-check to make certain your starter is alive and kicking (try some regular yogurtmaking), that sufficient time has transpired, and that the temperature was where it should be. If all appears to be well, try doubling the starter quantity, adding milk powder as directed (up to 3 tablespoons per quart) and/or reducing the amount of flavoring used.

Adding flavoring material after the milk has coagulated always involves stirring the curd to some degree. This tends to convert it to buttermilk. The solution is to mix dissolved, clear gelatin in with your flavoring. When the gelatin stiffens, the yogurt stiffens. Following this method, there is little you cannot add to the yogurt. Specific instructions are given following directions for flavoring prior to inoculation.

COFFEE YOGURT

1 quart lukewarm, weak coffee
2 cups milk powder, mixed with the above
2 tablespoons commercial starter (or 4 buttermilk)
Sugar or artificial sweetener to taste

Incubate at 86 degrees F., 10 to 14 hours, or at the temperature recommended for the culture you are using.

COFFEE YOGURT (alternate)

2 tablespoons commercial starter (4 of buttermilk)
1 quart whole milk
4 teaspoons instant coffee
Sugar or artificial sweetener to taste

159

Incubate at 86 degrees F., 10 to 14 hours, or at the temperature recommended for the culture you are using.

COFFEE YOGURT PARFAIT

3 standard 8-oz. glasses whole milk
1 standard 8-oz. glass light or medium sweet cream
3 tablespoons milk powder
2 tablespoons commercial starter (4 of buttermilk)
Sugar or artificial sweetener to taste
4 teaspoons instant coffee

Incubate at 86 degrees F., 10 to 14 hours, or at the temperature recommended for the culture you are using.

COLORED YOGURT

To make yogurt of any color simply add food coloring when mixing the starter with the milk.

FRUIT-JUICE YOGURT

3½ cups milk (whole or reconstituted skim)
½ cup fruit juice, any kind
½ cup milk powder
2 tablespoons commercial starter (4 of buttermilk)

Incubate at 86 degrees F., 10 to 14 hours, or at recommended temperature. Yogurt will be fruitlike in taste, but will be spongy if permitted to incubate too long. With pineapple juice, coagulum will be very spongy but edible. Reduce juice if appearance is disturbing.

FRUIT-FLAVORED YOGURT

1 quart milk—whole or skim
3 tablespoons milk powder
2 tablespoons commercial culture (4 of buttermilk)
2 tablespoons fruit flavoring—the kind used to make
 soda at home

Incubate at 86 degrees F., 10 to 14 hours, or at the temperature recommended for the culture you are using.

CHOCOLATE YOGURT

2 tablespoons commercial culture (4 of buttermilk)
1 quart whole milk
2 tablespoons standard chocolate syrup
3 tablespoons milk powder

Incubate at 86 degrees F., 10 to 14 hours, or at the temperature recommended for the culture you are using.

POSTINCUBATION FLAVORING

Yogurt can be flavored after it is chilled with fruit preserves, honey, wheat germ, maple syrup, chocolate syrup, or fresh fruit purees. Plain or herbed flavored yogurt can be used in salad dressings and as marinades for chicken, beef, and lamb.

TO ADD FRUIT

1 quart milk—whole or skim
3 tablespoons milk powder
2 tablespoons commercial culture (4 of buttermilk)

Incubate at 68 degrees F., 10 to 14 hours, or at the temperature recommended for the culture you are using. When the milk has coagulated, and before chilling, mix 1 envelope of clear, unflavored gelatin (Knox, for example, suitable for 1 pint of water) in ½ cup of warm water. When dissolved, mix gently into the warm yogurt. Add fresh or drained canned fruit. Chill.

TO ADD FRUIT (alternate)

Spread fruit on plate. Spoon yogurt gently on top of fruit.

11

CHEESE FORMULAS

Before we take off on our cheesemaking spree, let me repeat once more. Much of cheesemaking is still done by "feel" and much depends on the skill and experience of the cheesemaker. Don't expect to hit it right the very first time, or second or third time. And always keep a record. It is very likely you will discover a great new cheese, and if you don't remember how you did it, the world will cry with you. Don't believe it? Take my word for it; your cheeses are going to be different.

We have discussed milk, culture, coagulating, equipment, and procedures in previous chapters. If you have skipped directly to the back of the book, please return to the beginning and read it all. Without the background provided, I do not believe the formulas alone will be useful.

Please note that the same ratio of starter to milk is suggested for all formulas. When using commercial starter, time to coagulation at the recommended 86 degrees F. will be about 10 hours, perhaps, varying from 8 to 14 at the maximum. We hope that the use of commercial buttermilk as a starter will produce coagulation in the same length of time, but don't depend on it.

The commercial culture suggested is the strain or strains recommended by the lab for use in making a specific cheese. You can use yogurt cultures for making cheese, if you wish, but generally the results will be much too sour. See the Appendix for bacterial strains suitable for the various cheeses. Cream cheese is considered a fresh cheese and you can use strains developed for making cottage cheese, unless otherwise specified by the lab.

We have already discussed powdered milk, but let me repeat for clarity. *Powdered milk,* as listed in the formulas, means skim milk (1 percent milk-fat content) reconstituted by mixing the instant type of milk powder with water in the proportions recommended. The words *milk powder* appearing in the formulas means *additional* milk powder to be added in the quantity given.

The instructions, *permitted to coagulate and then held to the isoelectric point,* mean simply that the milk is held at incubation temperature until the curd is most firm, which of course is its isoelectric point as discussed in Chapter 5, "Coagulating."

CREAM CHEESE

Cream cheese is probably the easiest cheese to make. It is almost as simple to make as yogurt.

1. CREAM CHEESE

1 pint sweet cream
1 tablespoon commercial starter or 2 tablespoons
 buttermilk
¼ level teaspoon fine salt

Mix the sweet cream and starter. Make a muslin bag by tying the four corners of a large square of cloth. Pour the starter-cream mixture into the bag and hang up in a warm place to incubate and dry. Place a plate underneath as the bag may drip. Open bag 24 hours later. Cream should now be coagulated. If not, replace and check again 8 hours later, and again until cream has coagulated. Mix salt in after coagulation. Hang for further drying if a stiffer cream cheese is desired. Or place in dish and cool.

Choice of cream will control butterfat content of final cheese. One pint of cream will produce about ¼ pound of cheese, depending on how dry you let it get. Light cream will result in cheese with an approximate fat content of 32 percent.

2. CREAM CHEESE

1 pint sour cream (approximately 32 percent
 milk-fat content)
¼ Salada rennet tablet
¼ level teaspoon fine salt

Dissolve rennet in 2 tablespoons cold water. Mix well with sour cream. Place sour cream in double boiler and heat slowly to about 100 degrees F. Hold temperature 20 minutes. Remove from heat; let cool. Place in muslin bag. Hang in cool place to drain. When sufficiently dry for use add salt and refrigerate. Yield is about the same, approximately ¼ pound of cheese.

165

3. LOW-FAT CREAM CHEESE
(approximately 16 percent milk fat)

½ gallon whole milk
4 tablespoons commercial starter or ½ cup buttermilk
2 tablespoons milk powder
½ level teaspoon fine salt

Add culture to milk; add milk powder, mix and incubate at 86 degrees F. Wait until curd reaches isoelectric point (total time may run from 8 to 14 hours, though the ratio of starter to milk has been programmed for 10 hours). Pour gently into muslin bag. Add salt. Hang to drain. Remove and refrigerate when cheese is as firm as you like it. Makes about 1 pound of cheese.

4. LOWER-FAT CREAM CHEESE
(approximately 10 percent milk fat)

½ gallon skim milk
½ cup milk powder
4 tablespoons commercial starter or ½ cup buttermilk
½ level teaspoon fine salt

Proceed exactly as above. Makes about the same amount of cream cheese.

5. FIRMER, LOW-FAT CREAM CHEESE
(approximately 16 percent milk fat)

½ gallon whole milk
½ cup milk powder
4 tablespoons commercial starter or ½ cup buttermilk
½ level tablespoon fine salt

Dissolve milk powder in whole milk. Add starter. Incubate at 86 degrees F. until curd reaches isoelectric point. Cut curd in ¼-inch cubes. Raise temperature slowly to 100 degrees F. Hold 30 minutes. Remove from heat. Line colander with one large piece of muslin. Pour curds gently into colander. Let cool and drain. Then work salt in. You can reduce amount of milk powder added if you wish a softer cheese. Like the other formulas beginning with ½ gallon of milk, this one also makes about 1 pound of cream cheese.

DEVONSHIRE CLOT

This is more of a thick cream than a cream cheese. It is very popular in Devon and parts of Cornwall, where it is used as often with salads and fresh fruit as for spreading on bread and toast. Two varieties are made, double-cream and single-cream. The major difference is in the milk-fat content.

6. DOUBLE-CREAM DEVONSHIRE CLOT
(approximately 60 percent milk fat)

Start with 1 pint heavy whipping cream. The original is made with cream that is 50 percent milk fat. Spread a sheet of well-washed muslin over the inside of your colander. Mix 1 tablespoon of commercial starter or 2 of buttermilk with the cream. Spread the cream over the cloth, using a spoon. Place in a room at about 70 degrees to 75 degrees F. Cover with a cloth to keep bugs off. Return every now and again and use the spoon to spread the cream that has collected on the bottom, up and onto the sides of the cloth-covered colander. You want to expose as much cream surface as possible. The top of the cream will air-dry, the bottom of the cream will drain through the cloth. About 12 hours later, or when sufficient moisture has drained off and the cream has a slightly sour flavor, it is ready. Spoon it onto a plate and shape with a knife. One pint makes about ¼ pound of clot.

7. SINGLE-CREAM DEVONSHIRE CLOT
(approximately 35 percent milk fat)

Start with 1 pint light sweet cream. Follow same procedure as above. You will have the same wonderful taste, but only a little more than half the fat. One pint makes about ¼ pound of clot.

8. BROWNED DEVONSHIRE CLOT
(approximately 35 percent milk fat)

Place 1 pint light cream in a large, flat cookie tin. Place pan in oven with door open. Bring contents of pan very slowly up to 180 degrees F. and hold until a brown, wrinkled skin forms over the surface. Let cool, then refrigerate for 24 hours. Remove clotted cream. Browned Devonshire clot has a somewhat granular texture and a cooked-nut-like flavor. Be careful not to burn it while cooking.

The original recipe called for unpasteurized, unhomogenized milk. which was permitted to stand in a shallow pan until the cream floated to the top. Light sweet cream works equally well.

FRENCH CREAM CHEESE

(Forgive me dear gastronomes if I treat French cheeses so lightly; but cream cheese by any other name is still cream cheese.)

1. FROMAGE BLANC
(approximately 16 percent milk fat)

This is the way cream cheese used to be made in France, and perhaps still is, if there are any backwater French farmers remaining. Whole milk is permitted to sour, then placed in a muslin bag for drainage. It is eaten with pepper and salt.

½ gallon whole milk
4 tablespoons commercial culture or ½ cup buttermilk

Mix milk and culture together. Incubate at 86 degrees F. until the isoelectric point is reached. (Remember Chapter 5, the Alth and the Renner techniques.) Place in muslin bag or muslin-lined colander and drain until desired consistency is reached. Makes about 1 pound of cheese.

2. FROMAGE À LA CRÈME

Same as above.

Remove from bag and serve with sugar and plenty of heavy sweet cream.

3. COEUR À LA CRÈME

Same as above, but place curd in a small muslin- or cheesecloth-lined heart-shaped wicker basket, thus shaping the cheese into a heart. (The French appreciate the power of language.) Chill and serve with fresh strawberries.

4. DEMI-SEL
(approximately 70 percent milk-fat content)

1 quart heavy sweet cream
2 tablespoons commercial culture or ¼ cup buttermilk

Mix cream and culture together. Incubate at 86 degrees F. until cream is curdled firmly. Remove to muslin bag or muslin-lined colander. Let curd drain until desired consistency is reached. Add fine salt to taste. Makes about ½ pound cream cheese.

COTTAGE CHEESE

Cottage cheese, a high-acid, small-curd cheese, is always made from skim milk. This means the milk must be/ permitted to incubate sufficiently to reach coagulation and the isoelectric point whether or not rennet is added. Although you can work with less than a gallon of milk, this minimum quantity is recommended because the curd must be cooked and mixed. If you wish to work with more or less milk, change the formula proportionately. For ½ gallon use half the starter. For 2 gallons use twice the starter. Time and temperature remain the same, of course.

1. COTTAGE CHEESE
(approximately 4 percent milk fat)

1 gallon skim milk
½ cup milk powder
½ cup commercial starter or 1 cup buttermilk

Incubate at 86 degrees F. until the milk coagulates and reaches its isoelectric point. Cut into ¼-inch cubes. Hold 30 minutes at incubation temperature. Begin cooking and mixing; raise temperature slowly to 104 degrees F.; cook at this temperature 30 to 60 minutes. Test curd by removing and chilling a small sample. Continue cooking and raising the temperature if necessary. If curd remains weak at 115 degrees to 120 degrees F., drain whey and replace with warm water at same temperature. Continue cooking, going as high in temperature and cooking for as long as needed to get firm curd (as indicated by chilling sample). Remove from heat. Rinse in lukewarm water several times. Chill and salt to taste. Makes 1 to 2 pounds of cheese.

2. COTTAGE CHEESE
(approximately 4 percent milk fat)

1 gallon skim milk
½ cup milk powder
½ cup commercial starter or 1 cup buttermilk
1/16 Salada rennet tablet

Incubate at 86 degrees F. Remove ½ cup of mixture for use with AC test (see Chapter 5). Add rennet, dissolved in ¼ cup cold water. Hold at incubation temperature until test sample coagulates. Cut into ¼-inch cubes. Hold at incubation temperature 30 minutes. Begin cooking and mixing. Raise temperature slowly to 104 degrees F. Cook at this temperature 30 to 60 minutes. Test small sample of curds by chilling in cold water. If necessary, continue cooking and slowly raising temperature. If curd is still weak at 115 degrees to 120 degrees F., drain whey; replace with warm water at same temperature. Continue cooking, slowly raising the temperature until spongy-bodied curd is produced. Remove from heat. Rinse in lukewarm water several times. Chill and salt to taste. Makes 1 to 2 pounds of cheese.

3. CREAMED COTTAGE CHEESE

Proceed as above, using either method. When curds have been chilled and salted, cream is added. Use as much of any type as you desire. You can use regular sour cream, sour cream thinned with milk, or whole-milk yogurt, shaken or stirred to make it a liquid.

The curds by themselves are rather bland. The "cream," when it is sour, provides the tang. If you wish a sour cream not as thick as regular sour cream or as thin as yogurt, mix a little yogurt with sour cream to thin it out.

Cheese can be sweetened with sugar and vanilla extract and served with pureed fruits or flavored with pimento, chives, or assorted vegetables.

POT CHEESE

Pot cheese is known as a large-curd or sweet-curd cheese. Always made from skim milk, it is well-washed, like cottage cheese, but unlike cottage cheese, pot cheese does not go all the way to acid coagulation. Rennet is used to stop the action somewhat short of the high-acid level common to cottage cheese. On the average, the yield is somewhat higher, roughly 1¼ to 2 pounds of cheese per gallon of milk.

1. POT CHEESE
(approximately 4 percent milk fat)

1 gallon skim milk
½ cup powdered milk
½ cup commercial starter or 1 cup buttermilk
1/8 Salada rennet tablet

Mix skim milk, extra powder, and starter together. Incubate at 86 degrees F. Mix rennet in ¼ cup cold water; add to milk 5 hours after start of incubation. Use the Alth or Renner test to pinpoint the best time to cut curd, which will be roughly 1½ hours after rennet is added. Cut into 3/8-inch cubes. Hold at incubation temperature 30

172

minutes. Then begin raising the temperature slowly to 104 degrees F., mixing carefully as you go. Cook at this temperature 30 to 60 minutes. Test a few curds by chilling. If more cooking is needed, raise temperature to 115 degrees to 120 degrees F. If still more cooking is indicated, replace whey with water of the same temperature. Continue cooking and mixing, raising the temperature if necessary. When curds are sufficiently firm, remove from heat, wash well in lukewarm water, chill, and salt to taste.

FARMER CHEESE

Farmer cheese is a moderately acid, moderately washed, and lightly pressed cheese that falls somewhere between cream cheese and pot cheese. It can be made with or without rennet, from whole milk or a combination of whole and skim milk. When made from whole milk, the milk-fat content of the finished cheese is about 28 percent. When made from equal parts of whole and skim milk, the resultant cheese has a milk-fat content of about 1 percent. These figures remain true whether or not rennet is used. The addition of rennet makes for a slightly firmer, less sour cheese. Farmer cheese may be eaten fresh or aged. When it is to be aged, rennet is used and the cheese is pressed more heavily to reduce its moisture content. A gallon of milk produces about 1¼ pounds of finished cheese.

1. FARMER CHEESE
(approximately 28 percent milk fat)

1 gallon whole milk
½ cup milk powder
½ cup commercial starter or 1 cup buttermilk

Mix milk, extra powder, and starter together. Incubate at 86 degrees F. When curd reaches its isoelectric point cut into 3/8-inch cubes. Hold at temperature 30 minutes. Begin slow mixing and raising of temperature to 104 degrees F. Cook 30 to 60 minutes. If curd is not firm, continue to cook, slowly raising the temperature. Test curd by chilling samples from time to time. When cooking is complete, wash the curd thoroughly in lukewarm water. Drain, chill, and salt to taste. Then shape curds either by using hoop or wrapping in cloth and flattening a bit.

2. FARMER CHEESE—FIRMER
(approximately 32 percent milk fat)

1 gallon whole milk
½ cup milk powder
½ cup commercial starter or 1 cup buttermilk
1/8 Salada rennet tablet

Mix milk, extra powder, and starter together. Incubate at 86 degrees F. Five hours later, dissolve rennet in ¼ cup cold water; add to milk. Cut into ¼-inch cubes when curd reaches its isoelectric point. Hold at incubation temperature 30 minutes. Start cooking process. Raise temperature slowly to 104 degrees F.; cook 30 to 60 minutes. Test curds by chilling samples from time to time. Continue cooking and raising temperature until curds are firm. Rinse in lukewarm water. Drain and salt. Place in hoop and press with moderate pressure. A gallon of milk yields about 1 pound of finished cheese.

MUENSTER

Muenster is a semisoft whole-milk cheese. You can, if you wish, cut the calories by making it with part skim milk, but the flavor suffers. And you can, if you wish, make Muenster with more milk fat by adding a little sweet cream to the milk you start with. A gallon of whole milk makes a little more than 1 pound of cheese with a fat content of about 28 percent. If you alter the fat content, just be certain that you do not alter the total volume of milk. In other words, if you wish to use 1 quart of light cream, mix it with 3 quarts of whole milk, so that you still have the gallon the formula calls for.

1. MUENSTER
(approximately 28 percent milk fat)

1 gallon whole milk
¼ cup milk powder
½ cup commercial starter or 1 cup buttermilk
¼ Hansen's rennet tablet or 2½ Salada rennet tablets
Salt

Mix milk, powder, and starter together. Incubate at 86 degrees F. Three hours later dissolve the ¼ Hansen's tablet in ¼ cup of cold water. Mix rennet into milk, stirring well about one minute. Use Alth or Renner method to ascertain isoelectric point. It should take about 30 minutes for coagulation to occur. Cut curd into ¾-inch cubes. Raise temperature of curd to 90 degrees F. Hold at this temperature for 2 hours. Slowly raise temperature to 104 degrees F. Mix curds carefully as you do so. Cook at 104 degrees F. until curds are firm. If 60 minutes of cooking at

104 degrees F. doesn't do it, raise temperature slowly and cook some more. When curds are ready, remove from heat, drain, wash, and cool. Salt to taste and place in hoop while still warm. Press moderately.

2. MUENSTER
(slightly sourer, same milk-fat content)

1 gallon whole milk
¼ cup milk powder
½ cup commercial starter or 1 cup buttermilk
1½ Salada rennet tablets

Mix milk, powder, and starter together. Incubate at 86 degrees F. Four hours later dissolve 1½ Salada rennet tablets in ¼ cup of cold water. Mix rennet into milk. Use Alth or Renner method to determine isoelectric point. Cut curd into ¾-inch cubes. Raise temperature of curd to 90 degrees F. Hold this temperature for 2 hours. Raise temperature slowly to 104 degrees F., carefully mixing curds. Cook at 104 degrees F. until curds are firm. Raise temperature and continue cooking if 60 minutes at 104 degrees F. doesn't give the desired results. When curds are ready, remove from heat, wash, drain, and cool. Caraway seed can be added to the drained curd for extra flavor. Salt to taste and place in hoop while still warm. Press moderately.

AMERICAN CHEESE

American cheese is a form of Cheddar, but softer, milder, and easier to make. After cream cheese, American is the most easily made. Generally, American is made from whole milk. You can use a little skim, but any more than

25 percent skim noticeably affects the flavor and texture. The cheese is a little harder when less milk fat is included. A gallon of milk makes up to 1 pound of American.

1. MILD AMERICAN CHEESE
(approximately 32 percent milk fat)

1 gallon whole milk
½ cup milk powder
½ cup commercial starter or 1 cup buttermilk
¼ Hansen's or 2½ Salada rennet tablets

Mix the milk, milk powder, and starter together. Incubate at 86 degrees F. Two hours later, dissolve the rennet in ¼ cup cold water and add to milk. Use the Alth or Renner method to determine the isoelectric point. Cut curd into ½-inch pieces. Hold at 86 degrees F. for 30 minutes. Take at least 30 minutes to raise temperature slowly to 104 degrees F., mixing as you go. Cook until curd is firm. Give it at least 60 minutes at this temperature before slowly raising the temperature. When ready, remove from heat, wash, drain, and salt to taste. Place curd in hoop while very warm. Use moderate pressure.

2. SHARP AMERICAN CHEESE
(approximately 35 percent milk fat)

1 gallon whole milk
½ cup milk powder
½ cup commercial starter or 1 cup buttermilk
¼ Hansen's rennet tablet or 2½ Salada rennet tablets

Mix the milk, powder, and starter together. Incubate at 86 degrees F. Three hours later, dissolve the rennet in ¼ cup cold water and add to milk. Use Alth or Renner method to ascertain the isoelectric point. Cut curd into ½-inch pieces. Hold at 86 degrees F. for 30 minutes. Raise temperature slowly to 104 degrees F., mixing slowly and carefully. Cook at this temperature until curd is firm. If not firm in 60 minutes, gradually raise temperature and continue cooking until curd is firm. Remove from heat, wash, drain, and salt to taste (use a little more than you did with the mild American). Place curds in hoop while still very warm. Use high pressure. Makes from ¾ to 1 pound of cheese. Age cheese to develop sharp flavor.

3. SHARP AMERICAN
(approximately 35 percent milk fat)

1 gallon whole milk
½ cup milk powder
½ cup commercial starter or 1 cup buttermilk
1½ Salada rennet tablets

Mix milk, powder, and starter together. Incubate at 86 degrees F. Four hours later, dissolve the rennet in ¼ cup cold water and add to the milk. Use Alth or Renner method to locate isoelectric point. Cut curd into ½-inch pieces. Hold at incubation temperature 30 minutes. Raise temperature slowly to 104 degrees F. Cook and mix at this temperature. If not firm in 60 minutes, raise temperature slowly and continue cooking until curd is firm. Remove from heat, wash, drain, and salt (use more than you did with the mild American) to taste. Place in hoop while still warm. Use high pressure. Makes a slightly more acidic cheese than method 2. Must be cured (aged) to develop sharp flavor.

The major difference between mild and sharp American is that the latter goes into the hoop slightly more acidic, and generally with a little more salt. Both the mild and the sharp may be eaten fresh and both may be aged, but the sharp, having more acid, will taste better when aged. Aging removes some of the cheese's moisture, causing the butterfat content of sharp American to be higher than mild American.

4. ORANGE AMERICAN

Proceed as above.

Dissolve a fraction of an annatto tablet in cold water. Let it soak for 30 minutes afterward. Add the color to the milk when you start inoculation. Never add it after adding the rennet.

Color can be added to any cheese by the same means.

CHEDDAR

Cheddar begins its life as a sharp American, same formula, same procedure, excepting the milk is permitted to go a wee bit further along the acid route. Initial cooking is the same, but then it is cooked a second time, pressed very hard, and aged as long as your patience lasts. Three years is not too much, but Cheddars as young as 6 months (and possibly less) are sold commercially. It is supposedly best when made from the milk of the English shorthorn cow, but American-cow milk also works fine. You can use some skim, but whole milk produces better flavor.

1. CHEDDAR
(approximately 50 to 60 percent milk fat)

1 gallon milk
½ cup milk powder
½ cup commercial starter or 1 cup buttermilk
¼ Hansen's rennet tablet or 2½ Salada rennet tablets
2 tablespoons coarse salt

179

Mix milk, powder, and starter together. Incubate at 86 degrees F. Add color if you want an orange-tinted cheese. Three and one-half hours later, add dissolved rennet. Use Alth or Renner technique to determine isoelectric point. Curd is cut into ¼-inch cubes. Hold at incubation temperature 30 minutes. Then slowly raise temperature to 104 degrees F. Start mixing. Give curds 60 minutes at 104 degrees F. If not firm, raise temperature a little more and continue cooking and mixing. When curds are nearly firm, remove from heat and pour off the whey, leaving the curds in bottom of pot. Adjust water temperature to 105 degrees F. Add cold water if necessary; salt curds. Cover pot. Inspect every 15 minutes. When curds have melted into one lump, cut the lump into 1-inch or smaller pieces. Pour off the whey that appears. Curds should now be firm. Rinse in lukewarm water, drain, add salt to taste, place in hoop while still warm. Use very high pressure.

Cheddar, like American, can be eaten fresh, but it only develops its sharp flavor with aging. The best is aged 3 years, but even a few months will show a difference. With experience you may get ¾ pound of cheese to the gallon of milk, but at first your yield will be closer to ½ pound.

ITALIAN CHEESE

1. PROVOLONE

1 gallon whole milk
1 Hansen's rennet tablet or 2½ Salada rennet tablets

Heat milk to 86 degrees F. Dissolve rennet in ¼ glass cold water and mix with milk. When coagulated firmly, cut curd into ¾-inch pieces. Raise temperature as high as your hands can take it. Form curds into one solid lump and remove same from whey (do not discard whey). Place curd in hoop and press until firm. Return curd, still in hoop and cloth, to whey. Raise temperature of whey until it almost boils. Shut off heat and wait until everything is cold. Remove cheese. Let it drain 24 hours. It is ready to be eaten.

2. GRATING CHEESE

Follow recipe and procedure above. Rub drained cheese with fine salt. Let it remain in cool place until dry. Make ½ gallon of brine solution by slowly mixing salt into water; keep adding salt and mixing until no more salt will dissolve and salt collects on bottom. Store cheese in solution for about 4 days. Then remove the cheese and dry it again by rubbing it down with salt. Repeat salt rub and turn cheese over every few weeks. Cheese is ready in 4 to 6 months.

3. RICOTTA

1 gallon fresh whey (collected and saved from past cheesemaking sessions)
3 pints whole milk
½ cup strong vinegar

Heat whey until a cream forms on top; add milk, stir, and heat to near boiling. When curds appear, add vinegar. Continue stirring and heating (do not let it boil). Skim curds off. Place in cloth-lined colander for draining. After about 8 hours, curd may be salted to taste and is ready to eat.

12

STORING, PRESSING, AND DRYING

The fresh cheeses—cream, cottage, and pot—are not pressed nor dried in the sense that American or Cheddar is dried. They are eaten and enjoyed fresh. Should they need to be stored for more than a few days, select a pot with a tight-fitting cover of a size that will permit you to fill it to the brim. This done, cover it promptly. The less air, the less opportunity for our moldy friends to get at it.

I find that homemade fresh cheese can easily be kept twice as long without loss of flavor as can the store stuff. Generally, these cheeses do not go bad in the sense they develop a bad taste. What usually happens to them is that they become covered with mold; some green, some red, some even purple. Keeping the cheese covered delays the onset of mold. Supposedly, you can scrape the mold off and keep on eating. Maybe one can, but personally, I haven't got the guts.

As with mother culture, you can extend the life of your stored fresh cheeses by keeping them as cold as possible without freezing and by eliminating unnecessary air contact. If you plan to have a bit, remove only that quantity of cheese, but leave the balance covered. It is better to discard a little cheese once in a while than let the whole batch stand about and possibly be forced to discard most of it because of mold and bacterial growth.

Cream, cottage, and pot cheeses are not pressed in the sense that Farmer and other cheeses are. Whatever pressure they are subjected to is mainly the result of their own weight.

Traditionally, Farmer cheese has been shaped into long flat ovals. Roughly the cheese may be 1 foot long, 5 inches wide, and about 2 inches high. You can achieve this shape by simply spreading a clean, well-washed piece of muslin

The traditional way. How to form Farmer cheese into the shape usually encountered in shops selling this kind of cheese in so-called loose form.

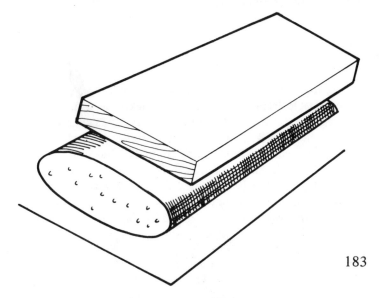

on the top of your table and spooning the curds into a long pile down the center of the cloth. The cloth is folded over, and a light board is placed atop it. This gives it the desired shape, as shown in the accompanying drawing.

One point to remember when doing this; the cloth acts to draw moisture from the cheese. Should your cheese be overly moist, you can draw off some whey by this method. But should your cheese contain just the amount of moisture you like, it is best to remove the cheese from the cloth so soon as you have shaped it. Then eat it or store it in a plastic bag in the refrigerator. If you let the cheese remain in contact with the cloth and leave the cloth exposed to the air in your room or in the refrigerator, drying—moisture removal—will continue.

To make firmer Farmer cheese than is possible with the rolled-cloth method, and to make all the other cheeses firm—normally they are pressed to varying degrees—you have got to go the bandage or the hoop-and-follower route. Bandaging a cheese is an old American custom. I prefer the hoop-and-follower method, but you may not. So here is how we bandage a cheese.

Pressing. Approximate weight of cheese and size of cheese obtainable from a single gallon of milk. The variation in weight is due to the care with which the curds are cooked and the amount of moisture lost by pressing or high heat.

One secures as much cheese using the 5-inch hoops as the 4, but the shape is different. When the cheese is to be cured, the best shape is nearly as high as it is wide.

If you double the amount of milk, you will naturally get twice the weight and cheeses twice as high or thick. Note that more pressure is necessary with the larger hoop.

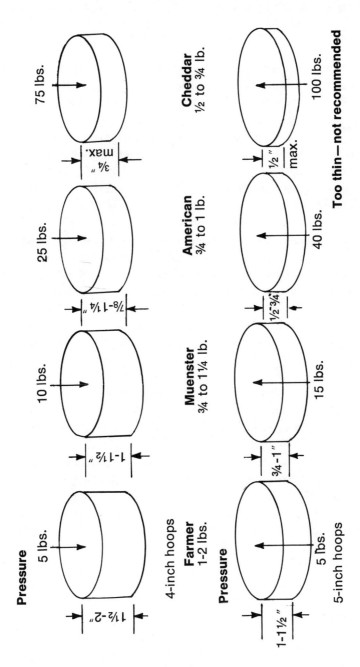

Pressure

5 lbs.	10 lbs.	25 lbs.	75 lbs.
1½-2"	1-1½"	⅞-1¼"	¾" max.
Farmer 1-2 lbs.	**Muenster** ¾ to 1¼ lb.	**American** ¾ to 1 lb.	**Cheddar** ½ to ¾ lb.

4-inch hoops

Pressure

5 lbs.	15 lbs.	40 lbs.	100 lbs.
1-1½"	¾-1"	½-¾"	½" max.

Too thin—not recommended

5-inch hoops

~150 lb

~60 lb

6"

185

Firstly, estimate the size of your cheese to be. If this is your first time around, see the accompanying figures, which are based on the use of 1 gallon of milk and hoops for shaping.

Let us assume we are making Muenster, and that we will form the curds into a 4-inch-diameter short cylinder. We need a piece of well-washed muslin 18 to 20 inches long and at least 4 inches wide, two brass safety pins and two squares of muslin 4 inches by 4 inches. If you are neat, cut the squares of cloth into two circles 4 inches in diameter.

We can do the American cheese bandage routine with or without a guide. It is easier when you have the guide, but not absolutely necessary. Anyway, let us sidetrack a moment and discuss the guide as illustrated in the accompanying figure.

As you can see, it consists of a couple of boards plus a couple of short dowels. Use oak for the top and bottom, if you can get it, and hardwood dowels. For the cheeses that we are going to make, the boards can be 1-inch thick and about 6 by 8 inches in width and length and the dowels, 1-inch in diameter. Drill holes for the dowels in the bottom board first. Cut two 1-inch holes about 6 inches apart with a drill; they must be well defined, so do not cut them out with a penknife. Reduce the diameter of the ends of two lengths of 1-inch dowel by sandpapering the ends. Then glue them home with waterproof cement. If you don't reduce the dowel ends so they fit easily, you may split the board while forcing them in and there will be no room for glue. Now drill two 1¼-inch holes in the second board in line with the two dowels and you have it.

Back to the bandage. Place one circle or square of muslin on the board between the dowels, or on your tabletop if you haven't made a guide. Take the long piece

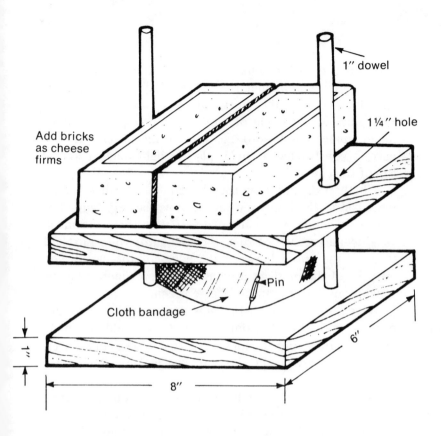

1" dowel

1¼" hole

Add bricks
as cheese
firms

Pin

Cloth bandage

6"

1"

8"

The bandage bit. The cheese curds are held in a circular shape by the length of cloth pinned in a circle. Pieces of cloth separate the top and bottom of the curds from the boards. When using this method, start with very light pressure; otherwise the curds will ooze out of the bandage.

Use 1-inch-thick dowels for the vertical guides and oak for the top and bottom boards, if you can get it. Glue the dowels into snug holes. Make the top holes oversize for easy passage. The boards are about 6 by 8 inches and the dowels about 6 inches apart. Nothing is critical.

As the cheese firms up, add pressure with weights—bricks, old pieces of silver, coins, anything handy, until you have the recommended weight and pressure.

187

of cloth and fold it lengthwise. Form it into an on-edge circle 4 inches in diameter. Use the safety pins to hold the ends together. Fill the short cloth tube with cheese curds. Place the second circle of cloth on top. Next, lower the upper guide board onto the top of the cheese. If you haven't constructed a guide, place a lightweight plate on top of the cheese.

Whether or not you use the guide, the first weight placed atop the bandaged cheese must be very light. Use the board alone or a light plate. If you apply too much weight and pressure at first, the soft curds will squirt out through the space between the edges of the cloth. You must build the pressure up gradually, never increasing the weights any faster than the cheese permits.

If you have a guide, the pins will keep the top board parallel with the bottom and you can add as many weights—bricks, old sections of railroad track, horse shoes, etc.—as you may need to bring the weight up to the figures indicated.

If you have not troubled to construct a guide of some sort, you need to keep checking the press to make certain the cheese hasn't tilted. This won't happen if you use very light weights at first. But get a little anxious and over she goes.

As you can imagine, if you are not planning to make any cheese firmer than soft Farmer, you will not need a guide. If you are trying for a harder cheese, however, you'll have a lot of watching and cheese-weight balancing to do, unless you use a guide.

Before leaving the bandage method of shaping a cheese, let me advise you of one advantage. You can, if you wish, wax a bandaged cheese with the cloth in place. This provides greater physical protection than the wax alone and permits earlier waxing. You do not need as thick a rind as you would without the cloth and therefore the cheese itself is not dried as long and usually, it is a little moister than an identical cheese waxed without cloth.

I prefer the hoop-and-follower method, however. Hoops and followers are easier to make and use, though the top of the cheese comes out somewhat uneven.

I use 1- and 2-pound empty coffee cans. The 1-pounder makes a 4-inch hoop; the 2-pound can makes a 5-inch hoop. The tops of the cans are cut open as cleanly as possible. Sandpaper is used to remove any burrs that remain. The smaller can is cut to get a section about 4 inches high; the larger can's sides are cut to a height of about 3 inches. Do not use ordinary scissors; they will be ruined. Instead, use regular tin snips or a pair of geared tin snips. Make the edge a bit wavy to allow the whey to drain out. There is no need to make holes in the sides of the can. Smooth the cut edge with sandpaper.

The followers are cut from wood. They need not be perfectly circular, but you cannot use squares because the cheese will slip by. If you can find a strong plate of the correct size, that will do just as well. The maximum diameter (I am assuming you will not cut a perfect circle) should be about ½ inch less than the diameter of the can to permit the cloth to pass.

To use, the cut edge of the can is placed on a strong plate. The cloth, a piece of well-washed muslin, about 15 by 15 inches, is spread across the bottom and up the sides of the can. The curds are dumped in, made smooth with a spoon, covered with the balance of the cloth, which is folded smooth and the follower placed on top. Next go the weights, and you can use about one-third of the total weight immediately. The curds cannot ooze out with this

Hooping it. The curds are washed in the colander, then gently transferred to the cloth-lined metal hoop. This is a good time to taste the curd to see if more salt is needed.

method. But, as stated, the top of the cheese will show the imprint of the folded cloth. Later, pressing done, you can use a sharp knife to make the surface smooth.

With the curds either in the bandage or in the hoop and the weights applied, pressing begins. The first few minutes will be the wettest, so stick around. If you are using the guide, you will need to wipe up the excess. If you are using the hoop and plate as directed, remove the weights and pour off the whey, then replace the weights.

Following up. After the edges of the cloth have been folded smoothly across the top of the curds, the follower is positioned.

The temperature of the pressing room is not critical, but a cool room, around 50 degrees F., is best.

It is now a matter of time and pressure. If you wish to accelerate drying, place a large dry cloth under the cheese. This will draw moisture from the bottom.

Again we have a situation that appears simple and straightforward, but actually is not. Pressing, the weight, and the time under weight have considerable effect on the "character" of the finished cheese. You cannot ruin the cheese now, but you can vary the results to a considerable degree by the amount of pressure you use and the length of time you use it.

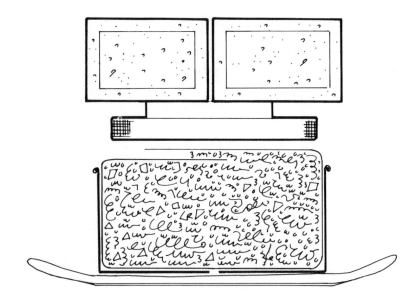

Meanwhile, on the inside. To explain further about hoops and followers, here is a cross section of the inside. The follower must be fairly close in size to the inside of the hoop, otherwise some of the curds are going to slip up and out. The block of wood on top of the hoop has to be smaller than the follower because the curds you see here are going to squeeze down to one-half or even less in height. Without the small block of wood, the bricks on top are going to rest on the hoop.

When it is to be eaten fresh, Farmer cheese is shaped simply by folding within a cloth as described, or by placing in a bowl, which is then inverted onto a plate. When Farmer is to be cured, it is pressed lightly. Muenster is pressed a bit more firmly. American is pressed fairly hard and Cheddar hardest of all. The diagrams on page 185 suggest approximate weights to be used with the various cheeses. Note that more weight must be used when the diameter of the cheese is larger.

Pressing is more than a matter of weight. The way the weight is applied is also important. You must begin with a fraction of the total weight. If you place the full weight on Farmer or Muenster while the curds are still soft, they will collapse and you will lose whey. You will not have as much trouble with the American or Cheddar, but moister cheese and greater total cheese yields will result if you work up to maximum pressure in several stages.

Time is also important, since the combination of pressure and time is what does the job properly. High pressure over a short period of time will not work. And if you permit a high pressure to remain too long on a cheese, you will get a drier than usual product.

Roughly, with the pressure suggested, give Farmer cheese a few hours, Muenster about six, the Americans about twelve, and the Cheddars about twenty-four hours.

When you have pressed a sufficient number of cheeses to have the weights and times down to a science, you can relax about the pressing operation. Until then you will need to make periodic checks on progress. This may be done by removing the weights and lifting the upper cloth a little, and peeking. Incidentally, the cloth will be sopping wet at first. This is normal.

If any cheese has squished past the upper cloth, use a

sharp knife to cut it off and taste it. If there are no "squishes" and you are working with the hoop, carefully fold the cloth back and use a sharp knife to slice some of the roughness from the top. It is not advisable to do this with the smooth surface normal to the bandaged cheeses. Generally the tiny bits you cut off are drier and firmer than the balance of the cheese, but they will indicate roughly its condition.

When the cheese bandage is no longer sopping wet, you can assume that the cheese itself (the cloth is always wetter than the cheese) is fairly dry. Remove it from the press and try its "character" by pressing on it with your finger. If it is as firm as you wish, it is ready for drying.

When examination indicates that the hooped cheese is ready, push it carefully down and free of the hoop. Then very, very slowly and carefully, pull the cloth off. Try your best not to peel any of the cheese off as you remove the cloth. You need that rind.

In order to develop the pressure needed for the Cheddar without building a mountain of weights, you will need an old wine press or some sort of lever system. You can make the latter fairly easily from a length of board, a bucket filled with old coins or just plain rocks or sand, a couple of large nails, and a block of wood.

The accompanying illustration indicates the general arrangement of parts. The "cleat" can be a length of thick wood; a 2 x 4 is fine. This is nailed to the basement wall or inside a closet where it will be out of sight. It is vital that the board be fastened firmly, so try a few nails in the wall first to make certain you locate the studs, which are the vertical pieces of wood inside the walls. If you have an open wall, they will be obvious.

Lacking a convenient wall but having a workbench that

is fastened firmly to the floor or is very heavy, fasten a large C-clamp to one leg in place of the aforementioned cleat. Another method involves screwing a large screw eye into the floor, and "tying" the end of the lever down with a loop of wire.

When using the lever, remember that the closer the bucket is to the cheese, the lower the pressure. Moving the bucket to the end of the lever increases the pressure.

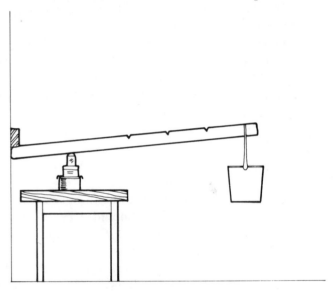

The press. If you recall your high school physics, you will remember levers. Now you can use the information. Fasten a cleat to the wall, position your cheese as shown, along with anything that will serve as a lever—a bed slat is fine. If the top of the cheese is 1 foot from the wall and the bucket of water, iron, sand, rocks, etc., is 5 feet from the wall, you get a pressure multiplication of 5, so 25 pounds in the bucket puts 125 pounds on the cheese. You need this much for Cheddar, but start with less pressure; start with the bucket close to the cheese.

When the cheese is pressed to our satisfaction and is as firm and moist as we wish, we need to dry it if we plan to cure it, that is to say, improve its flavor by aging.

Drying is the process of forming a solid rind. The rind serves several purposes, including keeping the moisture inside the cheese. Remember that even the hardest, firmest, driest Cheddar is moist. The rind acts to prevent the entrance of air and bacteria into the body of the cheese. When the cheese is to be waxed, the rind serves as a support. Wax will not adhere to a wet surface.

If your cheese has been bandaged, you have the option of leaving the cloth in place while you dry and then wax the cheese. (The cloth should not be left in place if the cheese is not going to be waxed. The cloth will become moist and provide an excellent haven for mold and other undesirables.) Or, you can carefully remove the cloth and dry the cheese.

If your cheese has been hooped, the cloth is carefully removed and the cheese is dried.

In either case, let us assume that the rind or skin on the cheese is not cracked or broken. (Should it be, additional steps must be taken prior to drying.) With a solid rind, all there is to drying is placing said cheese in a cool room and waiting until a dry rind forms, meanwhile, turning the cheese over every few days or so. To speed drying, we can place the cheese on a clean dry cloth. To ward off bugs and dust, I wrap my cheeses loosely in the cloth.

The extent of drying necessarily depends on your plans for the cheese. If you are going to wax, and wax is a necessity for prolonged storage, the cheese is ready as soon as its unbroken surface is dry to the touch. If you are going to store your cheese with only a rind, the rind must be drier and harder.

196

In addition to placing the cheese on a dry cloth, any number of methods have been developed over the centuries for forming harder, stronger rind more quickly. The purpose of the speed is twofold—first, to save time, but second and more important, to reduce interior drying. The sooner the rind becomes leather-like, the sooner moisture is sealed within the cheese.

One common method is to sprinkle salt on the cheese. To do this properly, a layer of salt is placed on a plate, the cheese is placed on top, and more salt is added. A variation consists of rubbing the cheese with salt. Still another consists of submerging the cheese in a brine solution.

Salt is hygroscopic. It draws water. Placed in contact with the surface of the cheese, the salt becomes moist and the surface of the cheese dry. For greater speed, wipe the wet salt off and replace with dry salt.

Very little of the salt works its way inward. Generally, you need not wait until a third or fourth application of dry salt no longer becomes wet. Usually, a heavy application of dry salt, its removal when wet, and one application and removal is all you need to form a good, hard rind.

You can use the salt-drying technique to firm a light rind on very soft cheeses such as cream cheese. It's a good way to store these if you've made too much. When the surface is dry to the touch, it can be waxed.

Other rind-development techniques consist of rubbing butter or olive oil into the rind. Some Italian cheeses are coated with a combination of olive oil and umber, a deep-brown earth color. For a black pigment, rub a combination of iron oxide and dilute sulfuric acid on the cheese. (This is used with Scanno.) Or rub it with a mixture of charcoal and salt. (Used on the rind of St.

Benoit, a French cheese.) Butter and olive oil, which of course can be used at home, are generally not used together. They hasten the drying and hardening of the rind. On the desert and other dry areas, the rind thus hardened serves as fair protection for the cheese. The rind alone is of little use in moist areas. As you must know from experience, mold will grow on a damp rind.

Should this happen to one of your cheeses, try rubbing the mold off with salt, which kills mold. If that doesn't work, try the hot salt water cure: Boil some water with about three tablespoons of salt per quart. Then use a spatula to lower your cheese into the boiling water. Let the cheese remain under water for about thirty seconds, then remove. The mold will be gone, and usually the smell associated with the mold will also have disappeared.

So far we have discussed the treatment of cheeses that were left in their bandage or were removed from their bandage or hoop cloth without any breaks in the still new rind. This is not always the case. Sometimes the surface of the cheese clings so tenaciously to the cloth, there is no way to free the cloth but to tear a strip of cheese loose.

In other cases, the upper surface of the cheese coming out of the hoop is so rough that you need to cut it smooth for appearance and waxing. In still other cases the cheese comes out of the hoop or from under the guide with cracks and sometimes with openings that leak whey.

Let us take the case of a simple break in the rind, where some has been torn away. This is corrected by using a sharp knife to make the edges of the break fairly level with the rest of the cheese. Where the original rind remains, the surface is fairly firm. Where the rind has been removed, the surface is comparatively moist. The treatment prescribed is the heavy application of salt to the wound. This will speed the drying of that area. When the damaged part becomes as hard as the rest of the surface, the cure is complete.

Deep cracks in the cheese are caused by too-dry, cold curds, by low pressure, or by insufficient time under pressure. The curds did not coalesce into a single mass. Nothing for it now, but if there is no moisture seeping out, ignore it. When you wax and later open the cheese you will have to pick bits of wax out from the crack. A nuisance, but nothing more.

If free whey or water appears at the crack, you have a problem. The curds were not dried sufficiently before hooping or bandaging, and in addition were probably cold at the time of forming. You now have a product made up of hard little bits of cheese with water in between. The best solution is simply to eat the cheese and forget about it. I have tried sealing these "wet" openings with a clean soldering iron. I melted the cheese over the hole. Sometimes it worked and sometimes it didn't. The important thing, of course, is to make certain you don't let this happen to your next cheese.

13

SEALING, CURING, AND PACKAGING

When the curds are pressed, most of the whey is removed. The percentage remaining varies with the type of cheese and the pressure used by the individual cheesemaker. Most of the bacteria that survived the cooking are to be found in the whey. Thus, the more whey is retained, the more bacteria are retained, with their potential for continued acid development. This is why the fresh cheeses and even Muenster, which retains a relatively large percentage of whey, continue to grow more sour with the passage of time.

Hard cheeses retain far less whey, and though they grow more sour with time, the increase is usually not noticeable. There is, however, a definite change due to enzymatic action. This is called the curing process and results in a "sharp" flavor.

While the curing process is actually very complex, we can consider it from a simple point of view. The lactic acid, which restricts the growth of contaminating microorganisms during cheesemaking and ripening, produces a proteolytic enzyme, which breaks down the cheese protein into simpler, water-soluble compounds. Milk fat is converted to fatty acids by hydrolysis. The lactose, citrates, and other organic substances form acids and aroma compounds. The quantitative change depends on time and temperature. That is to say, the higher the temperature and the longer we wait, the greater the enzymatic change that results.

However, the change is only accomplished in the absence of air. Were air to be present, putrefactive organisms would interfere and alter the results. In non-technical language, we would say the cheese is spoiled (mold-ripened cheeses excepted).

It is therefore necessary that we protect our cheese from air by one means or another. One method is the formation of a very tough, hard rind. Another is sealing off from the air by mechanical means. The importance of an airtight seal cannot be overstressed.

If you are a cheese "hound" you know how good a freshly cut piece of cheese tastes. You also know that the same piece of cheese, exposed to the air for a few hours or so, loses its flavor and becomes little more than food.

You can store cut or opened cheese very carefully and there are all sorts of fanciful tales about magic plastic boxes, and the use of cloth soaked in port wine. But if you have tried any of these methods, you know they do not offer protection. They merely delay the onset of flavor deterioration; they do not prevent it.

All this is stated to point up the importance of sealing a

cheese that is to be cured. Unless the cheese is perfectly sealed from the air, all the enzymes in the world will not help its flavor. (Mold-ripened cheeses are, of course, another matter.)

Cheese may be sealed in several ways. The simplest and least effective way is to use a plastic bag. The cheese is inserted into a bag, the bag's sides pressed close, and a knot made and slid down as close to the body of the cheese as possible. If the outside of the plastic bag is made wet, the knot can be slid close more easily. To open, the bag is slit with a knife.

Bagging cheese in plastic. This is what can be done with an ordinary plastic sandwich bag when it is knotted tightly, the knot slipped down as far as it will go, and as much air as possible pushed out by flattening. Though not as good as the wax, because the plastic is not perfectly airtight, it has its uses.

Use the heaviest bag available. Clear ones are best. Use two bags, one inside the other, for better results.

Although some air does pass through the bag with time, this method has several advantages. It is fast, inexpensive, and, most important, you can see what goes on inside. If there is an air leak and some mold starts spreading, you can open the bag and remove the mold. Rub the cheese with salt or dip it into boiling salt water.

Commercial cheese houses use heavy plastic bags which they seal with a bit of wire. The bags are more closely shaped to the cheese. You can try your hand at this if you wish.

The cheese is inserted into the bag. The bag is folded around the cheese, then the edges of the fold are melted together with a lukewarm pressing iron or soldering iron. This isn't easy because if the iron is too hot, the plastic melts and if not hot enough, the plastic won't soften. You need a temperature that softens the plastic just enough to make it stick. The best approach, I have found, is to use a layer of paper beneath the iron. Don't let any of the plastic melt onto the iron. If you do, you'll have a heck of a job removing it.

With enough care and practice, you will learn to seal the bag fairly close to the surface of the cheese. The overall appearance is much neater than the knotted arrangement.

Waxing is the traditional and best method of sealing cheese. It is simple, fast, and inexpensive, but it requires the surface of the cheese to be perfectly dry.

The easy way is to dedicate an old pot to the wax. Fill it with four or five pounds of lump wax, which can be purchased for about fifty cents a pound at a craft shop. Turn the heat to moderate. Let the wax melt and add one or two color tablets. They are small, but they work well.

Waxing cheese. Sealing the cheese in wax is the best method known. It makes a perfectly airtight and moisture-tight seal; but the surface of the cheese must be dry.

Use hot wax and remove the cheese almost immediately after dipping. If you pause, the cheese will warm up and will push the wax off, even if the surface of the cheese is dry.

(When finished waxing, simply let the wax remain there in the pot; that is why I said dedicated.)

Wait until the wax is melted. Use a stick to spread the color evenly. The wax should be hot, but not so hot you cannot put a finger in a little way.

You can dip any cheese that has a dry outer surface, and you can dip any cheese in a dry bandage, and any cheese that is in a dry bag. The procedure is the same in all cases.

Take hold of the cheese, dip half of it into the molten wax and remove immediately. You don't want the cheese to warm up. Move the cheese away from the pot of wax and heat. Let the wax on the cheese cool. If you do not get a definite, thin layer of wax, the wax is too hot. If the wax forms a thick layer, the wax is too cold. If you can see a space between the wax and the cheese or if moisture appears on the bare surface of the cheese, the cheese is too moist to be dipped. Aim for a thin, smooth layer when you dip.

Wait until this thin layer cools and solidifies, then turn the cheese in your hand and dip again. Repeat, but move your hand so that you do not dip the exact same section of cheese each time. Keep dipping and cooling until you have about one-sixteenth of an inch of wax on the entire surface. You need this much for strength.

The cloth-covered cheese is handled the same way. However, the cloth soaks up more wax so you do not need to dip as many times to get a satisfactory layer.

Once waxed, the cheese is perfectly sealed from the air. If you notice a pin hole, which can be caused by water or dust, take a small stick and drip some hot wax on the spot.

We mentioned dipping a "bagged" cheese. This is done with round cheeses which would be hard to hold otherwise. It also provides a stronger barrier than the bandage or the rind alone, and the bag method can be used with cheese that has a slightly moist outer surface. For example, a cream cheese ball that has been partially dried by adding salt to its surface.

Once again we call on the aid of that well-washed muslin. This time it must be perfectly dry, or the wax won't stick. Use a square and hold the ends together with a bit of wire—a paper clip tied with the aid of a pair of pliers will do fine. Just dip it into the wax, being certain to dip all of the bag, top as well as bottom. If it is too long for your pot's depth, turn it over and dip the dry end in.

Once the cheese is sealed from the air, there is little to do but wait and turn it over every few weeks. Any temperature under 70 degrees F. will do, but best results are obtained in the 50 degree to 60 degree F. range. The cooler the better, though the speed of curing is slowed.

Most of the change occurs during the first few months, so you can really call your cheese aged if it is ninety days old or more. Some shops call cheese that is more than sixty days old, aged. However, if you want real, top-grade Cheddar, three years is not too long. Most hard Cheddars sold in shops are about one year old, and if you find a Cheddar with a "soapy" sort of taste, it is supposedly due to forcing. The curing temperature was too high.

You may find it helpful and interesting to make a string of the same cheeses and store them for varying periods of time. This will help you judge whether or not the increase in sharpness, which comes only with age, is worth the wait.

Once the cheeses are sealed, moisture or dust on the outside are unimportant. Just keep turning them faithfully to keep whatever whey is present from collecting on the bottom of the cheese and remaining there.

The waxed cheeses are possibly the most attractive. Placing a waxed cheese in a plastic bag improves its appearance in the minds of some cheese fanciers. The bagged and waxed cheeses look rather exotic when hung from rafters by a string.

I label all my cheeses, even those I store for personal consumption. For one thing, it is easy to forget the type of cheese inside the wax and the time it was stored. For another, they make nice gifts.

I use a section of cardboard—the bottom of a glazed paper pie plate is just right. I cut a circle and make it adhere to the waxed cheese by heating the wax a bit, then pressing the cardboard on. I use a mailing tag on the bagged cheeses and rubber cement to make the labels stick to the plastic bags. The cement doesn't hold perfectly, but the cardboard will stick if it is not forced off.

You have come to the end of the instructions and are ready to start making cheese. You know pretty much what it's all about, but you don't know everything. Nobody knows everything there is to know about cheesemaking. There is still quite a bit of mystery left. But you aren't completely ignorant and you aren't working blind, which amounts to the same thing.

Good luck!!

May your curd always be firm, and may your cave forever be free of phage.

Appendix

Addresses

Salada Foods, Inc.
    Woburn, Massachusetts
    01801
Chr. Hansen's Laboratory, Inc.
    9015 West Maple Street
    Milwaukee, Wisconsin
    53214
International Yogurt Company
(Rosell culture in the United
  States
    628 North Doheny Drive
    Los Angeles,
    California 90069
Rosell Institute, Inc.
(Rosell culture in Canada)
    1000 Bedard Boulevard
    Chambly, Quebec, Canada
(For additional addresses of
culture suppliers contact your
state department of agriculture.)

Products (and prices at this
  writing)

Chr. Hansen's supplies
    Yogurt culture
    Acidophilus yogurt culture
    Acidophilus culture
      $2.25 per packet,
      2 grams, postpaid.
Dri-Vac lactic cultures
    2-gram vial, $3.00 each,
      postpaid
    1-4-5-6-8-9-10-12-15
    18-40-41-42-43-44-45
    51-52-53-54-55-56-57
    58-60-70-72-73-75-82
    188-253
Dri-Vac specialty cultures
    2-gram vial, $3.75 each,
      postpaid
    Yogurt CH-1, CH-2
    Citric acid fermenters
    (CAF)

(The names and addresses are given above for those who cannot purchase these supplies in their local drugstores or health-food shops.)

Lactobacillus casei
Lactobacillus
acidophilus
Lactobacillus bulgaricus
Lactobacillus helvecticus
Streptococcus
thermophilus (GH, B,
& F) AH
Propionibacterium
shermanii (PS-1)
NOTE: Hansen's collection of specialty cultures is too extensive to be listed here in its entirety. If there are special cultures not listed herein, please write the laboratory for more information.
Cheese rennet tablets
Package of 25, $3.05, postpaid

Cheese color tablets
Package of 12, $1.25, postpaid
International Yogurt Company supplies
Yogurt culture
Kefir culture
11-gram packet, $2.25 each, postpaid
Yogurt tablets
Write for current prices.
Yogurt face cream concentrate
Yogurt face and baby powder
Yogurt incubator
Rosell Institute supplies
Yogurt culture
Lactic cultures (cheese)
Write for current prices.
Salada supplies
Rennet tablets
Write for current prices.

Recommended applications for various cultures (Hansen's)

Product list
1—Cheddar, Monterey, and similar cheese.
2—Colby, stirred, Brick, Muenster, and similar cheese.
3—Cottage cheese, Cream cheese, Bakers cheese.
4—Buttermilk, sour cream,
5—Yogurt.
6—Italian, Swiss.
7—Blue mold-type cheese.

210

Culture list

(Any culture listed at the left by number can be used to make any product listed at right by number)

Dri-Vac® Lactic Cultures
(October, 1972)

To obtain the best possible results with a given Dri-Vac culture, please refer to the following information:

Dri-Vac Number	Recommended for the Following Products	Activity of Culture
1	1,3	X
4	1,2,3	X
5	3	X
6	1,3,4	X
8	2,4,7	XX
9	3,4	XX
10	3,4	XX
12	1,2,3,4	X
15	1,4	XX
18	1,4	XX
40	1,2,3,4	X
41	1,2,3	X
42	1,2,3	X
43	1,2,3	X
44	1,2,3,4	XX
45	1,2,4	X
51	2,4	X
52	7	XX
53	1,2,3,4	X
54	1,2,3	XX
55	1,2	XX
56	1,2,3,4	XX
57	2,4,7	XXX
58	1,2,3	XX
60	1,2,3,4	XX
70	1,2,3,4	XX
72	1,2,3	XX
73	1,2	XX
75	1,2,3	XX
82	1,2,3,4	XX
188	2,7	X
253	1,2,3,4	XX
GH	6	XX
AH	6	X
L. bulg	6	X

The above groupings for culture use are presented as a guideline based upon general experience. You may find that certain cultures can be used satisfactorily in categories other than those indicated for the cultures.

Instruction in the event of an attack by phage

Often we are asked for a suggested culture rotation based upon their phage relationships. The following is one such rotation. However, one can never be assured that this rotation or any other will guarantee or prevent starter failures due to phage. Adjustments may be necessary depending upon performance of individual starters in your particular operation.

Rotations for Hard-Type Cheeses
60-253-70-54-92-72-53-44-91-56-73-58-75-57
or:
8-91-70-57-72-92-75
or:
54-60-56-91-70-72-253-92-75

The above rotations are suggestions based upon phage characteristics and general experience. You may find a successful rotation series that differs with the above suggestions. If so, stick with it as long as you continue to receive good results. The important fact to remember is to *use different starter cultures every day or every round*. A rotation using the most individual cultures will give added assurance to a successful program.

Rotations are usually more critical for hard-type products, such as those listed in Groups 1 and 2. For cottage cheese production, etc., a selection of cultures recommended for Group 3 based on the proposed rotation presented above would be acceptable. You may find a different sequence which gives good results. *(Courtesy, Chr. Hansen's Laboratory, Inc., October 1972)*

Calories and Carbohydrates Found in Yogurt and Cheeses

Food and Description	Measure or Quantity	Calories	Carbo-hydrates (grams)
YOGURT:			
Made from whole milk (USDA)	½ cup (4.3 oz.)	76	6.0
Made from partially skimmed milk (USDA)	½ cup (4.3 oz.)	62	6.4
Plain:			
Swiss style (Borden)	5 oz. (by wt.)	94	9.9
Swiss style (Borden)	8 oz. (by wt.)	150	15.9
Swiss style (Borden)	5 fl. oz.	105	12.2
Swiss style (Borden)	8 fl. oz.	167	19.4
(Breakstone)	½ cup	74	6.1
(Breakstone)	1 T.	9	.8
(Dannon)	½ cup	65	7.0
(Sealtest)	½ cup	72	6.1
Apricot (Breakstone)	½ cup	143	26.9
Apricot (Dannon)	½ cup	130	25.8
Banana (Dannon)	½ cup	130	25.8
Black cherry (Breakstone) *Swiss Parfait*	5-oz. container	184	34.1
Blueberry (Breakstone)	½ cup	142	26.9
Blueberry (Dannon)	½ cup	130	25.8
Boysenberry (Dannon)	½ cup	130	25.8
Coffee (Dannon)	½ cup	100	16.8
Mandarin orange:			
(Borden)	5 oz. (by wt.)	152	28.7
(Borden)	8 oz. (by wt.)	243	45.9
(Borden)	5 fl. oz.	168	32.2
(Borden)	8 fl. oz.	268	51.4
Peach:			
(Borden)	5 oz. (by wt.)	149	27.8
(Borden)	8 oz. (by wt.)	238	44.5
(Borden)	5 fl. oz.	163	31.1
(Borden)	8 fl. oz.	261	49.6
Peach melba (Breakstone) *Swiss Parfait*	5-oz. container	191	36.0

(USDA): United States Department of Agriculture

213

Food and Description	Measure or Quantity	Calories	Carbo-hydrates (grams)
Pineapple (Breakstone)	½ cup	143	27.3
Pineapple-orange (Dannon)	½ cup	130	25.8
Prune whip (Breakstone)	½ cup	142	26.9
Prune whip (Dannon)	½ cup	130	25.8
Raspberry:			
(Borden)	5 oz. (by wt.)	158	29.5
(Borden)	8 oz. (by wt.)	252	47.2
(Borden)	5 fl. oz.	174	33.1
(Borden)	8 fl. oz.	278	52.9
(Breakstone)	½ cup	142	26.9
(Dannon)	½ cup	130	25.8
Strawberry:			
(Borden)	5 oz. (by wt.)	152	27.8
(Borden)	8 oz. (by wt.)	243	44.5
(Borden)	5 fl. oz.	166	31.3
(Borden)	8 fl. oz.	266	50.0
(Breakstone)	½ cup	143	27.3
(Breakstone) *Swiss Parfait*	5-oz. container	191	36.0
(Dannon)	½ cup	130	25.8
Vanilla:			
(Borden)	5 oz. (by wt.)	158	28.4
(Borden)	8 oz. (by wt.)	252	45.4
(Borden)	5 fl. oz.	173	31.9
(Borden)	8 fl. oz.	276	30.9
(Breakstone)	½ cup	101	15.0
(Dannon)	½ cup	100	16.8

CHEESE:

American or cheddar:

Natural:

Food and Description	Measure or Quantity	Calories	Carbo-hydrates (grams)
(USDA)	1″ cube (.6 oz.)	70	.6
Diced (USDA)	1 cup (4.6 oz.)	521	2.8
Grated or shredded (USDA)	1 cup (3.9 oz.)	442	2.3
Grated or shredded (USDA)	1 T.	30	Tr.
(Borden)	1″ cube	70	.6
(Kraft)	1 oz.	113	.6
(Sealtest)	1 oz.	115	.6
Sharp cheddar (Gerber)	1 T.	50	1.5

214

Food and Description	Measure or Quantity	Calories	Carbo-hydrates (grams)
Process:			
(USDA)	1 oz.	105	.5
(Borden)	1 oz.	105	.5
(Breakstone)	1 oz.	105	.5
Loaf or slice (Kraft)	1 oz.	105	.5
(Sealtest)	1 oz.	105	.5
With Brick cheese (Kraft)	1 oz.	101	.5
With Monterey (Kraft)	1 oz.	101	.5
With Muenster (Kraft)	1 oz.	100	.5
Dried, sharp cheddar (Information supplied by General Mills Laboratory)	1 oz.	171	1.7
Asiago (Frigo)	1 oz.	113	.6
Bakers Special (Kraft)	1 oz.	110	7.2
Bleu or blue:			
(USDA)	1 oz.	105	1.0
(Borden)	1 oz.	105	1.0
(Foremost Blue Moon)	1 T.	52	Tr.
(Frigo)	1 oz.	99	.5
(Gerber)	1 T.	49	1.6
Natural (Kraft)	1 oz.	99	.5
(Stella)	1 oz.	113	.6
Bond-Ost, natural (Kraft)	1 oz.	104	.4
Brick:			
Natural (USDA)	1 oz.	105	.5
Natural (Kraft)	1 oz.	104	.3
Process, slices (Kraft)	1 oz.	102	.4
Camembert, domestic:			
(USDA)	1 oz.	85	.5
(Borden)	1 oz.	85	.5
(Kraft)	1 oz.	85	.5
Caraway, natural (Kraft)	1 oz.	111	.6
Chantelle, natural (Kraft)	1 oz.	91	.3
Cheddar (See American)			
Ched-ett, process, cold pack (Kraft)	1 oz.	85	2.1
Colby, natural (Kraft)	1 oz.	111	.6
Cottage:			
Creamed, unflavored:			
(USDA)	1 cup (8.2 oz.)	247	6.8

215

Food and Description	Measure or Quantity	Calories	Carbo-hydrates (grams)
(USDA)	1 T.	15	.4
(Borden)	1 cup	241	6.6
Lite Line, low fat (Borden)	1 cup	189	7.0
Tangy small curd (Breakstone)	4 oz.	115	2.8
Tangy small curd (Breakstone)	1 T.	14	.4
Tiny soft curd (Breakstone)	4 oz.	115	2.8
Tiny soft curd (Breakstone)	1 T.	14	.4
(Foremost Blue Moon)	1 oz.	30	.4
(Kraft)	1 oz.	27	.9
(Sealtest)	1 cup	213	5.1
Light n' Lively, low fat (Sealtest)	1 cup	153	6.6
Creamed, flavored:			
Chive (Breakstone)	4 oz.	115	2.9
Chive (Breakstone)	1 T.	14	.4
Pineapple (Breakstone)	4 oz.	132	2.9
Pineapple (Breakstone)	1 T.	17	.4
Pineapple (Sealtest)	1 cup	204	13.0
Spring Garden Salad (Sealtest)	1 cup	210	8.1
Uncreamed:			
(USDA)	1 cup (8.2 oz.)	200	6.2
(USDA)	1 oz.	24	.8
(Borden)	1 cup	200	6.2
(Kraft)	1 oz.	26	.6
(Sealtest)	⅓ cup	60	1.0
Pot style (Breakstone)	4 oz.	85	1.9
Pot style (Breakstone)	1 T.	11	.2
Skim milk, no salt added (Breakstone)	4 oz.	88	2.2
Skim milk, no salt added (Breakstone)	1 T.	11	.3
Cream Cheese:			
Plain, unwhipped:			
(USDA)	1 oz.	105	1.0
(USDA)	1 T.	55	.3
(Borden)	1 oz.	105	1.0
(Breakstone)	1 oz.	99	.4
(Breakstone)	1 T.	50	.2

216

Food and Description	Measure or Quantity	Calories	Carbo-hydrates (grams)
Glass or loaf (Kraft)	1 oz.	98	.6
(Sealtest)	1 oz.	98	.6
Plain, whipped (Breakstone):			
Temp-Tee	1 oz.	99	.4
Temp-Tee	1 T.	33	.2
Flavored, unwhipped (Kraft):			
With bacon & horseradish,			
glass	1 oz.	91	.5
With chive, glass or loaf	1 oz.	84	.8
With olive-pimento, glass	1 oz.	85	.8
With pimento, glass or loaf	1 oz.	85	.7
With pineapple	1 oz.	87	2.5
With relish, loaf	1 oz.	88	2.4
With Roquefort, glass	1 oz.	80	.7
Flavored, whipped (Kraft):			
Catalina	1 oz.	94	1.1
With bacon & horseradish	1 oz.	95	.7
With blue cheese	1 oz.	98	.7
With chive	1 oz.	92	1.0
With onion	1 oz.	93	1.5
With pimento	1 oz.	91	1.2
With Roquefort cheese	1 oz.	99	1.3
With salami	1 oz.	88	1.2
With smoked salmon	1 oz.	90	1.7
Edam (House of Gold)	1 oz.	105	.3
Edam, natural (Kraft)	1 oz.	105	.3
Farmer cheese, packaged			
(Breakstone)	1 T.	19	.8
Fontina (Stella)	1 oz.	113	.6
Frankenmuth, natural (Kraft)	1 oz.	113	.6
Gjetost, natural (Kraft)	1 oz.	135	13.0
Gorgonzola (Foremost Blue			
Moon)	1 oz.	110	Tr.
Gorgonzola, natural (Kraft)	1 oz.	112	.4
Gouda, baby (Foremost Blue			
Moon)	1 oz.	120	Tr.
Gouda, natural (Kraft)	1 oz.	108	.5
Gruyère (Gerber)	1 oz.	101	.5
Gruyère, natural (Kraft)	1 oz.	110	.6
Jack-dry, natural (Kraft)	1 oz.	102	.4

Food and Description	Measure or Quantity	Calories	Carbohydrates (grams)
Jack-fresh, natural (Kraft)	1 oz.	95	.4
Lagerkase, natural (Kraft)	1 oz.	108	.3
Leyden, natural (Kraft)	1 oz.	80	.7
Liederkranz (Borden)	1 oz.	86	.4
Limburger, natural (USDA)	1 oz.	98	.6
Limburger, natural (Kraft)	1 oz.	98	.6
MacLaren's, process, cold pack (Kraft)	1 oz.	109	.6
Monterey Jack (Frigo)	1 oz.	103	.4
Monterey Jack, natural (Kraft)	1 oz.	103	.4
Mozzarella:			
(Frigo)	1 oz.	79	.3
Natural, low moisture, part skim (Kraft)	1 oz.	84	.3
Natural, low moisture, part skim, pizza (Kraft)	1 oz.	79	.3
Muenster, natural (Kraft)	1 oz.	100	.3
Muenster, process, slices (Kraft)	1 oz.	102	.6
Neufchâtel:			
(Borden) *Eagle Brand*	1 oz.	73	1.0
Loaf (Kraft)	1 oz.	69	.7
Natural (Kraft) *Calorie-Wise*	1 oz.	70	.7
Swankyswigs (Kraft):			
Olive-pimento	1 oz.	70	1.2
Pimento	1 oz.	67	1.4
Pineapple	1 oz.	70	2.7
Relish	1 oz.	71	3.3
Roka	1 oz.	80	.6
Nippy Whipped (Kraft)	1 oz.	82	.9
Nuworld (Kraft)	1 oz.	104	.7
Old English loaf, process, slices (Kraft)	1 oz.	105	.5
Parmesan:			
Natural:			
(USDA)	1 oz.	111	.8
(Frigo)	1 oz.	107	.8
(Kraft)	1 oz.	107	.8
(Stella)	1 oz.	103	.9
Grated:			
(USDA)	1 cup (3.7 oz.)	416	3.0
(USDA)	1 T.	26	.2

Food and Description	Measure or Quantity	Calories	Carbohydrates (grams)
(Borden)	1 T.	26	.2
(Buitoni)	1 T.	22	1.5
(Frigo)	1 T.	27	.2
(Kraft)	1 oz.	127	1.0
Shredded (Kraft)	1 oz.	114	.9
Parmesan & Romano, grated:			
(Borden)	1 oz.	143	.9
(Borden)	1 T.	31	.2
Pepato (Frigo)	1 oz.	110	.8
Pimento American, process:			
(USDA)	1 oz.	105	.5
(Borden)	1 oz.	105	.5
Loaf or slices (Kraft)	1 oz.	104	.4
Pizza:			
(Frigo)	1 oz.	73	.3
(Kraft)	1 oz.	73	.3
Shredded (Kraft)	1 oz.	86	.4
Port du Salut (Foremost Blue Moon)	1 oz.	100	Tr.
Port du Salut, natural (Kraft)	1 oz.	100	.3
Prim-Ost, natural (Kraft)	1 oz.	134	13.0
Provolone (Frigo)	1 oz.	99	.5
Provolone or Provoloncini, natural (Kraft)	1 oz.	99	.5
Ricotta cheese (Sierra)	1 oz.	50	1.3
Romano:			
Natural:			
(Frigo)	1 oz.	110	.8
(Kraft)	1 oz.	110	.8
(Stella)	1 oz.	106	.6
Grated:			
(Buitoni)	1 T.	21	1.5
(Frigo)	1 T.	29	.2
(Kraft)	1 oz.	134	1.0
Shredded (Kraft)	1 oz.	121	.9
Roquefort, natural:			
(USDA)	1 oz.	105	.5
(Borden)	1 oz.	105	.5
(Kraft)	1 oz.	105	.5
Sap Sago, natural (Kraft)	1 oz.	76	1.7
Sardo Romano, natural (Kraft)	1 oz.	110	.8
Scamorze (Frigo)	1 oz.	79	.3

Food and Description	Measure or Quantity	Calories	Carbo- hydrates (grams)
Scamorze, natural (Kraft)	1 oz.	100	.3
Swiss, domestic:			
Natural:			
(USDA)	1 oz.	105	1.0
(Foremost Blue Moon)	1 oz.	105	1.0
(Kraft)	1 oz.	104	.5
(Sealtest)	1 oz.	105	.5
Process:			
(USDA)	1 oz.	101	.5
(Borden)	1 oz.	101	.5
Loaf (Kraft)	1 oz.	93	.5
Slices (Kraft)	1 oz.	95	.6
With American (Kraft)	1 oz.	99	.5
With Muenster (Kraft)	1 oz.	98	.6
Washed curd, natural (Kraft)	1 oz.	108	.6
CHEESE FOOD, process:			
American:			
(USDA)	1 oz.	92	2.0
(Borden)	1 oz.	92	2.0
Grated, used in *Kraft Dinner*	1 oz.	129	8.4
Slices (Kraft)	1 oz.	94	2.1
(Foremost Blue Moon)	1 oz.	87	1.5
With bacon (Kraft)	1 oz.	101	.7
Blue, cold pack (Kraft)	1 oz.	89	2.2
Cheddar, cold pack (Kraft)	1 oz.	90	2.4
Links:			
Bacon, garlic or jalapeño (Kraft)	1 oz.	93	2.2
Nippy (Kraft)	1 oz.	93	2.2
Smokelle (Kraft)	1 oz.	93	2.2
Swiss (Kraft)	1 oz.	91	1.4
Loaf:			
Munst-ett (Kraft)	1 oz.	101	1.7
Pimento *Velveeta* (Kraft)	1 oz.	90	2.5
Pizzalone (Kraft)	1 oz.	90	.5
Sharp (Kraft)	1 oz.	97	1.1
Super blend (Kraft)	1 oz.	92	1.6
Super blend with caraway (Kraft)	1 oz.	94	1.6
Velveeta, California only (Kraft)	1 oz.	90	2.5

Detailed Composition of Milks and Cheeses

	Food energy Cal.	Protein Gm.	Fat Gm.	Total carbo-hydrate Gm.	Cal-cium Mg.	Phos-phorus Mg.	Iron Mg.	Vita-min A value I.U.	Thia-mine Mg.	Ribo-flavin Mg.	Nia-cin Mg.	Ascor-bic acid Mg.
Milk, cow:												
Fluid (pasteurized and raw):												
Whole:												
1 qt.	666	34.2	38.1	47.8	1,152	908	.7	1,550	.35	1.68	1.1	13
1 cup	166	8.5	9.5	12.0	288	227	.2	390	.09	.42	.3	3
Nonfat (skim):												
1 qt.	350	34.4	1.0	50.2	1,210	954	.7	40	.35	1.75	1.1	13
1 cup	87	8.6	.2	12.5	303	239	.2	10	.09	.44	.3	3
Canned:												
Evaporated (unsweetened), 1 cup	346	17.6	19.9	24.9	612	491	.4	1,010	.12	.91	.5	3
Condensed (sweetened), 1 cup	981	24.8	25.7	167.7	835	698	.6	1,300	.16	1.19	.6	3
Milk, goat, fluid:												
1 qt.	654	32.2	39.0	44.9	1,259	1,035	1.0	1,550	.39	1.04	2.8	10
1 cup	164	8.1	9.8	11.2	315	259	.2	390	.10	.26	.7	2

Detailed Composition of Milks and Cheeses

	Food energy Cal.	Protein Gm.	Fat Gm.	Total carbohydrate Gm.	Calcium Mg.	Phosphorus Mg.	Iron Mg.	Vitamin A value I.U.	Thiamine Mg.	Riboflavine Mg.	Niacin Mg.	Ascorbic acid Mg.
Cream:												
Light, table, or coffee:												
½ pt.	489	7.0	48.0	9.6	233	185	.1	1,980	.07	.34	.2	3
1 tablespoon	30	.4	3.0	.6	15	12	.0	120	Tr.	.02	Tr.	Tr.
Heavy or whipping:												
½ pt. (approx. 1 pt. whipped)	779	5.4	82.6	7.6	184	144	.1	3,390	.06	.26	.1	1
1 tablespoon	49	.3	5.2	.5	12	9	.0	220	Tr.	.02	Tr.	Tr.
Half and half (milk and cream):												
1 qt.	1,322	31.0	116.2	43.6	1,045	823	.6	4,760	.32	1.52	1.0	12
1 cup	330	7.7	29.0	10.9	261	206	.1	1,190	.08	.38	.2	3
Butter:												
1 cup	1,604	1.3	181.4	0.9	45	36	0.0	7,390[2]	Tr.	0.02	0.2	0
1 tablespoon	100	.1	11.3	.1	3	2	.0	460[2]	Tr.	Tr.	Tr.	0
1 pat or square (64 per lb.)	50	.0	5.7	.0	1	1	.0	230[2]	Tr.	Tr.	Tr.	0
Buttermilk, cultured (from skim milk):												
1 qt.	348	34.2	1.0	49.8	1,152	908	.7	40	0.35	1.74	1.1	13
1 cup	86	8.5	.2	12.4	288	227	.2	10	.09	.43	.3	3

Cheese:												
Blue mold, domestic type, 1 oz.	104	6.1	8.6	.6	89	96	.1	350	.01	.17	.1	0
Camembert, 1 oz.	85	5.0	7.0	.5	30	52	.1	290	.01	.21	.3	0
Cheddar:												
1 cup, grated	446	28.0	36.1	2.4	812	554	1.1	1,570	.03	.47	Tr.	0
1 oz. (1-in. cube)	113	7.1	9.1	.6	206	140	.3	400	.01	.12	Tr.	0
Cheddar, processed, 1 oz.	105	6.6	8.5	.6	191	223 [2]	.3	370	Tr.	.12	Tr.	0
Cheese foods, Cheddar, 1 oz.	92	5.8	6.8	2.0	162	226	.2	303	.01	.16	Tr.	0
Cottage, from skim milk:												
1 cup	215	43.9	1.1	4.5	216	425	.7	50	.04	.69	.2	0
1 oz.	27	5.5	.1	.6	27	54	.1	10	.01	.09	Tr.	0
Cream Cheese:												
1 oz.	106	2.6	10.5	.6	19	27	.1	410	Tr.	.06	Tr.	0
1 tablespoon	56	1.4	5.6	.3	10	15	.0	220	Tr.	.03	Tr.	0
Limburger, 1 oz.	97	6.0	7.9	.6	167	111	.2	360	.02	.14	Tr.	0
Parmesan, 1 oz.	112	10.2	7.4	.8	329	233	.1	300	.01	.21	.1	0
Swiss, 1 oz.	105	7.8	7.9	.5	262	160	.3	410	Tr.	.11	Tr.	0
Swiss, processed, 1 oz.	101	7.5	7.6	.5	251	246 [3]	.3	390	Tr.	.11	Tr.	0

Bibliography

An American Cheese: How to Make It for Home Use. Farmer's Bulletin No. 2075. Washington: U.S. Department of Agriculture, 1954.

"Brainy Bacteria." *Time,* September 18, 1972, p. 63.

Bruthwell, D. and P. *Food in Antiquity.* New York: Praeger, 1969.

Byerly, T. C. *Livestock and Livestock Products.* Englewood Cliffs, N.J.: Prentice-Hall, 1964.

Cheese Varieties and Descriptions. Handbook No. 54. Washington: U.S. Department of Agriculture, 1969.

Daniel, G. *The First Civilizations.* New York: Crowell, 1968.

Frazer, W. C. *Food Microbiology.* 2nd ed. New York: McGraw-Hill, 1958.

Goodhard, R. S. *Nutrition for You.* New York: Dutton, 1958.

Home Economics, Foods and Cooking. 60th ed. Washington: U.S. Government Printing Office, 1972.

How to Make Cheese on the Farm and in the Home. Milwaukee: Chr. Hansen's Laboratory, n.d.

Judkins, H. F., and H. A. Keene. *Milk Production and Processing.* New York: Wiley, 1960.

Kretchmer, N. "Lactose and Lactase," *Scientific American,* October, 1972, pp. 71-78.

Lampert, L. M. *Modern Dairy Products.* New York: Chemical, 1965.

Layton, T. A. *Cheese and Cheese Cookery.* New York: World, 1967.

_____. *Choose Your Cheese.* London: Duckworth, 1957.

Lindsay, J. *The Ancient World.* New York: Putnam, 1968.

Making Cottage Cheese at Home. Home and Garden Bulletin No. 129. Washington: U.S. Department of Agriculture, 1967.

Marquis, V., and P. Haskell. *The Cheese Book.* New York: Simon and Schuster, 1965.

Morse, R. A. "Writing on Mead," *Scientific American,* September, 1972, pp. 185-190.

Nelson, J. A., and G. M. Trout. *Judging Dairy Products.* 4th ed. Milwaukee: Olsen, 1964.

Parker, D. *The Wonderful World of Yogurt.* New York: Hawthorn, 1972.

Patton, S. "Milk," *Scientific American,* July, 1969, pp. 105-109.

Peyton, A. B. *Practical Nutrition.* New York: Lippincott, 1962.

Phillips, R. W. "Cattle," *Scientific American,* July, 1958, pp. 51-59.

Sellars, R. L., and F. J. Babel. *Cultures for the Manufacture of Dairy Products.* Milwaukee: Chr. Hansen's Laboratory, 1970.

Seneca, H., E. Henderson, and A. Collins. "Bacterial Properties of Yogurt," *American Practitioner and Digest of Treatment,* Vol. I, No. 12 (December, 1950).

Simon, A. L. *Cheeses of the World.* London: Faber, 1951.

Von Haller, A. *The Vitamin Hunters.* Philadelphia: Chilton, 1962.

Watt, B. K., and A. L. Merril. *Composition of Foods.* Agriculture Handbook No. 8. Washington: U.S. Department of Agriculture, 1963.

Webb, B., and A. H. Johnson. *Fundamentals of Dairy Chemistry.* Westport, Conn.: Avi, 1965.

Whyte, K. C. *The Complete Yogurt Cookbook.* San Francisco: Troubadour, 1970.

226